Preface

Outline of the book

This book has been written assuming little previous knowledge on the part of the reader with regard to academic theories of power or theories of therapy. I have tried to be as clear as possible about academic constructs and to use everyday language to explain theoretical ideas. Despite this aim, however, some chapters are more theoretical/academic than others. In particular, Chapters 3 and 4 are quite dense in terms of describing theory. I have endeavoured to write each chapter to stand alone, referring to previous chapters where knowledge from these chapters is used. For those readers interested in theoretical concepts, Chapters 3 and 4 provide the basis of the theory that I have used. However, these chapters are not essential for a reading of the later, more practice-based chapters on models of therapy: it is possible to miss them out, going straight to later chapters and referring back to them as necessary to explain further the theory used in these chapters.

This book is for everyone who has an interest in, or experience of, therapy or counselling. It should be a useful textbook for qualified therapists and counsellors and students or trainees as an introduction to considering the ethics of power as therapists. It also aims to provide a theoretical framework for the analysis of the complex issues surrounding power. It should be useful for survivors of emotional distress who have used therapy or counselling, by providing information about models of therapy and a theoretical understanding of the dynamics of power. Certainly, learning about the theory and critiques of psychodynamic therapy helped me make sense of the discomfort I felt with my own sense of powerlessness as a client with a psychodynamic therapist. I hope it will be a useful resource for activists working to challenge the position of power of therapists within the mental health system, by providing a theoretical understanding to pre-empt and argue against the traditional justifications from the proponents of various models of therapy.

This book is an exploration of power in the therapy relationship. By 'therapy', I am referring to anyone who practises counselling or therapy in any context. By the 'therapy relationship', I am referring to the relationship between the counsellor/therapist and client. I use 'therapy relationship' rather than the more often used 'therapeutic relationship', as it certainly cannot be taken for granted that this relationship is 'therapeutic' or helpful.

My exploration is limited to the aspects of power in the therapy relationship within the therapy dyad, and external factors influencing the power relations will not be considered. Thus, I will not be considering the dynamics of power in the institutions of psychiatry or other contexts within which therapists practise. The added dimensions of power within the context of therapy provide more factors to consider which are beyond the scope of this book. However, I hope the analysis of factors within the therapy dyad will point to additional contextual factors. Thus, this book is relevant to therapists working in all contexts — for those working with private contractual arrangements directly between therapist and client, and for those working for institutions such as the NHS or other agencies. These various contexts will influence the aspects of power within the relationship, however, and need to be considered within the analysis of each aspect of power.

Chapter 1 introduces the topic of power and therapy by exploring the context of power within mental health in general and the relationship of powerlessness to psychological distress. I then consider power specifically in the therapy relationship. Of the literature on power in therapy, nearly all authors are critical of the power in the therapy relationship. Chapter 2 demonstrates how most of this literature does not consider the models used to analyse power relations. In Chapters 3 and 4 I explore all major models of power used from the disciplines of politics, sociology, philosophy and psychology, and investigate how these models inform and limit the literature on power in counselling. In Chapters 5, 6 and 7 I also examine three models of therapy and consider how these models theorise issues of power. My thesis is limited to a critique of theories of therapy, whereas the application of theories by individual practitioners and the practitioners' interpretation of the models are far more variable and flexible. However, if models of therapy are not practised in the way they are theorised, then the ways in which models are adapted to consider issues of power by individuals needs to challenge and change the theories. Finally in Chapter 8 I summarise the themes of the book and provide recommendations and checklists for therapists wanting to consider the dynamics of power in their own practice.

The Dynamics of Power
in
Counselling and Psychotherapy

Ethics, politics and practice

Gillian Proctor

PCCS BOOKS
Ross-on-Wye

First published 2002
Reprinted 2008, 2010, 2012, 2013

PCCS Books
2 Cropper Row
Alton Road
Ross-on-Wye
HR9 5LA
UK

T: +44 (0)1989) 763900
F: +44 (0)1989) 763901
W: www.pccs-books.co.uk
E: contact@pccs-books.co.uk

The Dynamics of Power in Counselling and Psychotherapy: Ethics, politics and practice

ISBN 978 1 898 05940 0

Cover design by Old Dog Graphics
Cover photograph by Sam Hughes
Printed by Ashford Colour Press, Fareham, UK

Contents

Acknowledgements

This book has its origins in a doctorate thesis on this subject that I submitted in 1999. My first thanks are to my supervisors for this original thesis: Wendy Hollway and Carol Sherrard. Thanks also to those with whom I discussed my ideas at this point and as a result of these discussions I was encouraged to refine my ideas and turn them ideas into a book, in particular, to David Pilgrim and to Clare Shaw. More recently, thanks to the many who have put in the time and effort to read various drafts of the book or specific chapters, and whose comments have enabled me to improve the final result particularly with respect to clarity, accessibility and hopefully interest: Claire Eady, Jerold Bozarth, Hamish Kemp, Derek Lawton, Carol Martin, Ian Parker, Jacqui Saradjian, David Smail, Wendy Spragg, Bernie Tuohy, Julian Turner and Sheila Youngson. Special thanks to those who provided comments for the back cover: Dorothy Rowe, Barbara Temaner Brodley and David Smail. I am very grateful to my publishers Pete Sanders and Maggie Taylor-Sanders for their agreement to publish, their support and encouragement. A final thanks to all my friends who have been constantly bored by my moaning about what stage I'm up to and everything I have had to do to get to this point; without their support and belief in me, it would have been a very lonely path.

Chapter 1

Why does power in therapy matter?

Power is an issue that is close to my heart for many reasons. Throughout my adult life, the principles of respect and value for each individual have been very important to me, and seeing people being disrespected has always made me angry. I have struggled with my own dilemma of feeling powerless and believing that I have enough worth and responsibility to be powerful. I have tried to work out how to feel empowered without using power over others. I have struggled in relationships to create mutuality and space for all to have their own power and not encroach on each other's power.

One way that I understand relations of power is through the model of how society is structured, such that various groups who differ from the 'norm' are defined as 'other' and set up by society to have less access to power. These groups (for example, women, Black[1] and minority ethnic people, working-class people, lesbians and gay men) experience oppression which includes being subject to stereotypes, assumptions and invalidation, reduced access to resources and often the real fear of violence and harassment. Smail (1987) explains that 'We live in a society in which enormous power is wielded to obscure enormous injustice'. I have experienced being oppressed on both a personal and an institutional level (because of being a woman and other aspects of my identity), and through these experiences I have become more and more aware of the structures of power in society. (See Chapter 3 for explanation and discussion of structures of power in society.) I have also become aware of my role as a potential oppressor with regard to other aspects of my structural positions (such as being White British) which place me within a group or groups holding structural power in my society.

As a psychologist in clinical training, I felt constantly uncomfortable with the power and expert status I was given in relation to clients coming for help with distress, and worried about how my position could so easily be abused. I struggled for two years to try to find a way of working with which I felt comfortable, with which I could aim towards establishing

---

1. Here I use the term 'black' as a political identity to include all who experience oppression because of colour, 'race' or ethnic background.

mutual relationships. At the same time, I began personal therapy as a client with a psychodynamic therapist, and felt increasingly uncomfortable and angry about the power dynamics in my therapy and how I felt my therapist used her power over me. (Chapter 7 describes this experience in more detail.) Finally, during a counselling course, I discovered person-centred therapy and found a model with which I felt personally and politically comfortable. In addition, my clinical work and theoretical understanding is now within the context of my feminist and socialist principles. It is from these contexts that my approach to power is informed.

In my research thesis for my MSc in clinical psychology, I investigated the experiences of lesbian clients of clinical psychologists (Proctor, 1994), and discovered that the main issue seemed to be that of power and how psychologists as therapists negotiated and used their position of power. So for my doctorate thesis I explored theories of power and how they could be applied to models of therapy. It was a huge relief to me to be able to explain theoretically the internal disquiet I had felt for so long about most models of therapy and 'expert' help.

The relationship of powerlessness to the experience of psychological distress

Power is a concept considered more often in disciplines of politics and sociology than in psychology and counselling. However, power and control and the experience of powerlessness are frequently mentioned in understanding all kinds of psychological distress. Finkelhor (1986) identifies four major dynamics following the experience of childhood sexual abuse: traumatic sexualisation, stigmatisation, betrayal and powerlessness. The experience of abuse is a significant causal factor in all types of psychological distress, with the numbers of survivors of abuse being very high among survivors of the psychiatric system (for example, Williams and Watson, 1994, suggest a figure of at least 50%). However, a diagnosis of psychiatric disorder is not the inevitable consequence of childhood adversity. Rutter (1990) charts the changing emphasis in research from vulnerability to resilience and suggests that this represents the move from a focus on risk variables (e.g. abuse) to the process of negotiating the risk situation. Rutter (1990) argues that protection 'stems from the adaptive changes that follow successful coping', not simply the avoidance of risk variables. Troop and Treasure (1997) examined the relation between childhood adversity and later experience of eating distress. They found that there was a higher rate of 'childhood helplessness' and a lower rate of 'childhood mastery' in women diagnosed with eating disorders. They concluded that it is not simply the presence of adversity in childhood that is a causal factor in the development of eating disorders, but the way in which these adverse experiences are negotiated. Clearly, the crucial determining factor in this negotiation is the woman's sense of power, which I would argue is at least partly determined by the woman's immediate relational context and wider social political environment in terms of women's role and power in society.

Other particular manifestations of psychological distress have also been strongly associated with issues of power and control. One of the functions of self-injury can be to feel more in control and cope with a feeling of powerlessness (Arnold and Magill, 1998; Spandler, 1996). Gilbert (1992) explains depression as a response to powerlessness, providing a more psychological model following the behavioural learned helplessness model of Seligman (1974). Byrne and Carr (2000) investigated the association between depression and power within marriage. They found that, in couples including a depressed woman, the woman's power bases (her economic and personal assets enabling her to have control over her partner) were financially and psychologically weaker. In addition, her ability to determine the outcomes in decision-making concerning household and childcare tasks was lower than her partner's and lower than non-depressed women. The experience of psychosis can be understood as not having control over one's sense of self and identity (see Johnstone, 1999). The experience of anxiety can be understood as being a result of fear about uncertainty and lack of control over one's environment, and so again is clearly related to a subjective feeling of powerlessness.

Structural positions of power and psychological distress

I would argue that the higher prevalence of members of oppressed groups in psychiatry reflects the positions of power of the groups involved. There is much evidence to associate the likelihood of suffering from psychological distress with the individual's position in society with respect to structural power. The higher rates of diagnosis for women compared with men of many disorders, such as depression, anxiety and eating disorders, reflects women's position in society with respect to power (see Johnstone, 1989; Baker Miller, 1991; Williams and Watson, 1994; Wenegrat, 1995). Yet the response by psychiatry to women is characterised by 'tending to *remove* power and control from the woman, to *deny* her feelings, and to *ignore* the meaning behind her actions' (Johnstone, 1989, p. 120).

Katzman (1997) argues that studying power differentials rather than gender differences would be more valuable for understanding the development of eating distress. She suggests that the predominance of women with eating disorders may more aptly reflect differences between men and women in the opportunity to establish self-definition and control. In addition, the higher rates of diagnosis of black and minority ethnic groups can be analysed in the same way (see Fanon, 1986; Mercer, 1986; Fernando, 1991).

Working-class people are over-represented in the mental illness statistics too (Gomm, 1996). Warner (1994) describes the triangular relationship between social and economic conditions, physical illness and psychological stress, with causality running in all directions. He also demonstrates clearly the causal link between the social and political climate and mental distress by showing that recovery rates from schizophrenia correlate with the state of the economy, leading him to argue that the development of psychiatry is governed by the political economy. Williams and Watson (1994) cite others who have argued that, when mental health professionals ignore the links between social inequalities and psychological distress, they serve the interests of privileged social groups rather than those of their clients.

As Smail (1987) states, clients of the mental health system are 'people upon whom the world has impinged in any of a variety of painful ways. They are less people with whom anything is wrong than people who have suffered wrong.' Clearly, the way to deal with difficulties that stem from abuse, deprivation and powerlessness is not to impose further power and control through the psychiatric system. The power of medicalisation serves to divert attention from the environmental causes of distress, the experiences of abuse, deprivation and powerlessness.

Given that power is such a key issue in the causes and experience of psychological distress, it is surprising that it is not considered more in models of helping distress. Psychiatric systems are set up around hierarchical systems of control and power; superficial and token ways of 'empowering' patients are sometimes considered briefly. Psychiatric systems are much more successful in controlling people experiencing distress than in helping to alleviate distress. Johnstone (1989, p. 116) notes that 'Sometimes the parallels between treatment and abuse are disturbingly close'.

Psychiatry and power and control

The anti-psychiatry (such as Laing and Szasz), and now 'post-psychiatry' (Bracken and Thomas, 2001), movements have critiqued the hierarchies of power within psychiatry since the 1960s–70s. Szasz (1997) draws a comparison between the mental health movement and the Inquisition, comparing the belief in witchcraft and persecution of witches to the belief in mental illness and the persecution of psychiatric patients. Cooper (1967, p. 12) described the 'violence *of* psychiatry'.

Szasz's main critique of psychiatry is of the coercive elements (the legal right of doctors to detain and treat patients without their consent) and the alliance of medicine and the state. He suggests that only when coercive psychiatry is abolished can the moral powers of uncoerced psychotherapy be released. Coercion includes not only the incarceration of people in psychiatric institutions against their will, but also the ascription of the role of psychiatric patient through diagnosis as opposed to individuals describing or assuming their own identities. Newnes and

Holmes (1999) similarly suggest that the future for mental health services must be to separate from the public protection function of coerced treatment and to provide services that people want and ask for when in mental distress.

However, even without coercion, people willingly offer themselves to psychiatry as a result of identifying their own distress in psychiatric terms. The power of the psychiatric system is not just in treating people against their will but also in the power of defining distress in terms of illness. The psychiatric system does not just have implications in terms of power and control on psychiatric patients, but affects all citizens by the threat of being labelled 'mad'. Laing explains, 'by and large psychiatry functions to exclude and repress those elements society wants excluded and repressed' (1985, p. 9). Miller and Rose explain psychiatry's role with regard to the management of society, saying

> The contemporary psychiatric system seeks not merely to eliminate mental illness, but to manage all aspects of life with the aim of producing and maintaining mentally healthy citizens. The production of socially competent and trouble-free psyches has become central to institutional efficiency, social tranquility and personal happiness. (1986, p. 5)

C. S. Lewis (1970) illustrates the effects of the rhetoric of medicine and helping used by psychiatry, saying 'Of all tyrannies a tyranny sincerely exercised for the good of its victims may be the most oppressive' (quoted in Breggin, 1993, p. 3). Laing (1985) also notes the power given to psychiatric staff by the law, and emphasises that this does not include the power to give this power away or back to the service user. He noted: 'I am still more frightened by the fearless power in the eyes of my fellow psychiatrists than by the powerless fear in the eyes of their patients' (quoted in Breggin, 1993, p. 3).

Power and responsibility

Johnstone (1989) explains how the functioning of the medical model in psychiatry sets up the dynamics of the 'rescue game'. When a patient needs help, the psychiatric system tries to help them (the rescuer helping the victim). However, when rescuing does not work, the rescuer begins to feel angry at the victim and switches to persecuting or punishing; conversely, the victim may feel angry at being treated as less than equal and persecute the rescuer. Transactional Analysis theory, in describing these roles, hypothesises that each player will occupy every position in the game at some time. Johnstone emphasises that none of these positions and dynamics can be a basis for relating to others as equals (see Fig. 1 over). The most common dynamic within the psychiatric system is of the mental

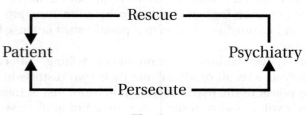

Fig. 1

health professional first attempting to rescue the client and then changing to persecution when rescue attempts fail. Or else, as is common particularly with women diagnosed with borderline personality disorder, the client is blamed and made to feel responsible for her behaviour and persecuted. Johnstone notes the particular likelihood of persecutory responses to people who self-injure, often reinforcing the self-hatred that contributed to their need to self-injure in the first place. With both rescuing and persecuting, the balance of power lies with the professional. Johnstone (1989) clearly demonstrates how this unhelpful dynamic of power is set up by the idea of the client/patient not being responsible and the professional taking responsibility for them. This is clearly demonstrated in the notion of the 'responsible medical officer' in charge of each patient's care. Service users report a dissatisfaction of being passive recipients of pejorative (blaming, judgemental and labelling) care (Sainsbury Centre for Mental Health, 1997).

However, Johnstone continues:

> Yet it is not enough to tell people they are responsible for their own problems and to dismiss them, as tends to happen in Persecution. Clearly, they are genuinely distressed and in need of some kind of help. What is needed is recognition that people suffering mental distress are responsible, capable agents and in need of help as well. (1989, p. 55)

Obviously, this alternative model is one in which the client's autonomy is promoted and respected while acknowledging and helping with distress in a way in which a client has requested. Johnstone also emphasises the true meaning of informed consent within this model. She explains:

> If the principle of informed consent were adhered to, it would be an important step towards turning the people who use the psychiatric services from patients — a word which implies the sick role, a passive waiting on expert advice — into clients who are actively selecting and participating in their own treatment. (1989, p. 59)

However, a change of attitude towards psychiatric patients still fails to address the broader socio-political context. Johnstone (1989) also notes that even with this change of approach, this still fails to address the discrimination and oppression attached to a psychiatric diagnosis. Similarly Bracken and Thomas (2001) suggest that the goal of post-psychiatry should be for social, political and cultural contexts to be central to our understanding of madness and that the voices of service users and survivors should be centre stage.

Johnstone (1989) clearly emphasises the social implications of diagnosis as well as the relational dynamics between professionals and clients. She points out that

> To give someone a diagnosis in psychiatry, unlike in general medicine, is to introduce them into a role and a life of stigma, social exclusion and discrimination which would be a struggle even for the emotionally resilient. (p. 63)

She emphasises that changing the way clients are treated in the psychiatric system involves participating in the political struggle against social injustice as well.

Power in therapy

In counselling and therapy, the legal position with respect to power is different from that held by a psychiatrist or psychiatric nurse. There is potentially more choice in how the therapist uses or chooses not to use the power given to them. However, as Sanders and Tudor point out,

> Just as it is dangerous to assume that psychiatry is a benign force in social policy or that Home Secretaries know anything about personality disorder, neither should we accept or assume that therapy is in itself benign, useful or effective. (2001, p. 157)

Miller, in Miller and Rose (1986), emphasises that 'we should be wary of celebrating psychological approaches as alternatives to psychiatry' (1986, p. 42). Psychological approaches can also be used as part of the armoury of power and control over the population, as Foucault particularly explains. Chapter 4 describes Foucault's and other post-structuralist approaches in more detail.

Aspects of power

I will consider three aspects to power in the therapy relationship, which I have clarified following DeVaris (1994). The first is the power inherent in the roles of therapist and client resulting from the authority given to the therapist to define the client's problem and the power the therapist has in the organisation and institutions of their work. I will call this *role power*. Whatever the context of a therapist's work, there is still power given by society to those identified as therapists. Various contexts of work can add to the authority given to the therapist (such as the NHS in the UK).

The second aspect of power is the power arising from the structural positions in society of the therapist and client, with respect to gender, age, etc. I will call this *societal power*. The final aspect of power in the therapy relationship is the power resulting from the personal histories of the therapist and client and their experiences of power and powerlessness. I will call this *historical power*. The personal histories and experiences will affect, and to some extent determine, how individuals are in relationships and how they think, feel and sometimes behave with respect to the power in the relationship. Throughout the book, I will demonstrate how these aspects of power in therapy have been addressed using various models of power and the three main models of therapy from which most other models are derived.

The three aspects of power that I consider are interrelated, and all apply to the relationship between the therapist and client, rather than residing within either individual. These dynamics can be represented by two triangles, one to represent the client and the other, the therapist. Each point represents the contribution from each individual to each aspect of power. So long as these triangles are separate and unconnected, they function separately, without integration, co-operation or domination (Fig. 2a). But the triangles can merge; for example, one triangle could absorb the other, which would represent complete domination (as in Fig. 2b). Alternatively, the triangles can integrate, with a large area shared by both triangles and representing mutuality in therapy (Fig. 2c). The unshared points of the triangles represent the parts of each individual that remain

Fig. 2a Separation   **Fig. 2b Domination**

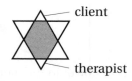

Fig. 2c Mutuality

unique. This book explores how therapy can aim towards as much mutuality as possible and represent the dynamics of power as in Fig. 2c.

Another useful way practically to conceptualise the relations of power in the therapy dyad is to consider Cromwell and Olson's (1975) domains of power. They theorise power in families as a construct incorporating three analytically distinct but interrelated domains: power bases, processes and outcomes. *Power bases* are the economic and personal assets (such as income, economic independence, control of surplus money, sex-role attitudes, desire for intimacy, physical and psychological aggression) that form the basis of one partner's control over the other. *Power processes* are interactional techniques, such as persuasion, problem-solving or demandingness, that individuals use in their attempts to gain control over aspects of the relationship. *Power outcomes* are who has the final say — who determines the outcome in problem-solving or decision-making.

These ways of conceptualising power will be used to apply to therapy in the rest of the book.

Chapter 2

Isn't therapy always dangerous or abusive?

Does power exist in the therapy relationship? There is much literature that concerns itself with an unequal power balance in the therapy relationship, and most that has been written about this inequality of power points to its adverse and dangerous effects. I argue that this literature is based almost exclusively on the modernist concept of power following the Hobbesian tradition (for details of Hobbes's theory, see Chapter 3). It is assumed that power is unitary, monolithic, unidirectional (held by the therapist over the client), structural (i.e. inherent in the roles of the therapist and client, or in their structural positions in society), and necessarily negative. There is also the occasional use of Arendt's concept of collective power or empowerment or the feminist concept of 'power-with' (for details of Arendt's and feminist theory, see Chapter 3), suggesting a more positive use of power but again based on structural assumptions of power as a possession. The notion of personal internal power or 'power-within' is referred to but generally dismissed (again, see Chapter 3 for explanation about feminist concepts of power). Some authors conclude that inequality of power is inherently avoidable and abusive in therapy, whereas others are more optimistic about working with this power in therapy. In this chapter, I demonstrate how the literature on power in therapy is founded on these modernist assumptions about power and confusion of different aspects of power. This limits the analysis of power and prevents the realistic consideration of power as inevitable and dynamic in all relationships. In addition, most of this literature makes generalisations about therapy without reference to the very different theories and assumptions within each model of therapy.

Power in the role of the therapist

The inequality of power is oppressive

Some authors point to the inequality of power in therapy and equate this with oppression and abuse. The most well-known proponent of this argument is Masson (1989). He explains this by saying :

> The therapeutic relationship *always* involves an imbalance of power. One person pays, the other receives. Vacations, time, duration of the sessions are all in the hands of one party. Only one person is thought to be an 'expert' in human relations and feelings. Only one person is thought to be in trouble. (p. 289, original emphasis)

Here the implicit notion is of power as a possession which only the therapist possesses. Masson's argument depends on the assumption that an imbalance of power is necessarily oppressive, and considers only the aspect of power in the roles of therapist and client.

This develops the argument that an imbalance of power is structured in the roles of the therapist and client. Bannister explains:

> The therapeutic situation involves an initially non-reciprocal relationship in which the balance of power lies with the therapist and which, thereby, is not a democratic situation . . . You may negotiate all things but you negotiate from a position of power. (1983, p. 139)

Here again, power as a possession is implicit. However, Bannister believes that this 'initial' unequal relationship can change to become more equal, and in fact he suggests that this should be the aim of therapy. He explains:

> 'Cure' can be defined as reaching a level at which the client can effectively contest the psychotherapist's view of life, i.e. the level at which the client does not need psychotherapy or the psychotherapist. (ibid.)

Here, although Bannister begins with the thesis that power in therapy represents the structures of power in society, which is negative, he then suggests that the therapy dyad can change these structures in that relationship; that the client can gain power so it is no longer held only by the therapist. Here the notion of internal or personal power is confused with the notion of structural power, and it is suggested that an imbalance in structural power can be remedied by an increase in the client's internal power.

The authority of the therapist is also demonstrated by the idea of the beneficent therapist, who knows what is best for the client and who has the authority to define reality. Dorothy Rowe (1989) says: 'In the final analysis, power is the right to have your definition of reality prevail over other people's definition of reality'. She explores power in the therapy relationship in the context of the foreword for Masson's *Against Therapy* (1989), and she continues:

> Many people who wish to impose their definition of reality would deny they are involved in gaining power. They would say that because of their greater knowledge, wisdom, training and experience they know what is best. The most dangerous people in the world are those who believe they know what is best for others. (pp.16–17)

Implicit in her definition is the concept of power as domination or control, as unidirectional — possessed by one person, the other being powerless. Here, the implicit assumptions of the negativity of power and the sole consideration of 'power-over' are clearly demonstrated.

Masson emphasises the danger inherent in the power of the therapist's role, given by the authority and expert status attached to this position. Theories of therapy provide therapists with assumptions, values and attitudes that make it more likely for issues of misuse and abuse of power to occur. Spinelli (1998) argues that the heart of potential abuse arises from theories that suggest a sense of knowledge, leading therapists to listen through the filters of theory and dismiss what does not fit. Here again, it is assumed that the therapist alone possesses power, although there seems to be some assumption that power may not be used negatively. Masson (1989), on the other hand, suggests that the effects of the therapist's expert status are the therapist's control and exploitation of the patient. He points out that:

> Therapists certainly expect their patients to look up to them . . . In any area of disagreement between the patient and the therapist, it is assumed that the therapist is more likely to be right (more objective, more disinterested, more knowledgeable, more experienced in interpreting human behaviour) than is the patient (p. 41)

He further explains that, although therapists may say they are attempting to do what will benefit the patient,

> It sounds good, but can we really expect this kind of impartiality and tolerance from a therapist? . . . The attempt to impose one's own views on patients goes against the canons of most forms of therapy. But in reality that is what most therapists do. (p. 42)

Further, 'A prison warden, a slave holder, and a psychotherapist have in common a desire to control another person'.

Some authors claim that the therapist's authority inevitably leads to abuse of power. Masson catalogues the abuses of Rosen, a prominent therapist in the USA, and asks: 'Is Rosen an exception, or is there something about psychotherapy, that tends towards such abuses?' (p. 189). He then answers his own question by pointing to the prevalence of sexual exploitation of patients by therapists and concluding:

> When we look at the evidence . . . we see case after case where psychotherapy in actuality, has abused and harmed people in concrete ways. It is true that we always have the option of saying that these cases represent exceptions . . . But at what point do we begin to see that there must be something about psychotherapy itself that creates the conditions that make such abuse possible? (p. 211)

Masson is much more adamant than Spinelli that power is always used oppressively, and assumes that the client is completely powerless. He points to the evidence of widespread sexual exploitation by therapists, particularly the evidence of Chesler (1972), who discussed the regularity of the sexual abuse of women in therapy relationships. He provides evidence for instances where power or control have harmed those who have been controlled, and then assumes that, whenever power is used, it is always harmful and oppressive. He further assumes that therapists are motivated to harm people, and allows for little possibility of therapists who want to use their power in ways that are helpful to the client. Furthermore, he makes no distinction between the various models of therapy and allows no space for models, such as person-centred therapy, where the expert status of the therapist is challenged.

The structural power inherent in the therapist's role

Other authors criticise the power inequality in therapy by demonstrating the control or influencing of clients by therapists in the therapy situation. Cooke and Kipnis (1986) examined taped therapy sessions (although the model of therapy was undefined) and classified the therapist's interventions with respect to various 'influence tactics' defined as any attempt to change a client. This is an example of a particular exploration of 'power processes' used in therapy, as defined by Cromwell and Olson (1975). These tactics included instruction, explanation, focusing, verbal reinforcement and support, including encouragement and interruption. All therapists demonstrated the use of these 'influence tactics' and the type of tactics used changed, from the beginning to the end of the session, with an increase in the use of more active forms of influencing. Again, the assumption implicit in their model of influence or power is that this is negative and oppressive — and also unidirectional, since the clients' parts of the conversations are not similarly analysed to see if they are attempting to change the therapist. Also, the client is assumed to be powerless, and there is no analysis of how clients might resist the therapist's control. The implicit assumption seems to be that this form of interaction and influence is unique to therapy and is not prevalent in all conversations and relationships.

Language

Further evidence for the presence of an unequal power relationship is provided by the examination of language used in the therapy encounter. Johnstone (1997) looks at the characteristics and consequences of the therapist's use of jargon in therapy. She notes that jargon, a specialised language, gives the impression of expertise and authority and thus promotes the power differential in the relationship. She also points out that using jargon can be a way to avoid disagreement by the client, in that the client's behaviour can be interpreted as part of their pathology or problems. Also, jargon can be used to justify punitive practices, a point previously made by Masson, who points out that, under the guise of 'expert', any behaviour can be justified as being in the best interest of somebody. Sherrard (1999) further demonstrates the inequality in the therapy relationship through the examination of language used by psychologists to describe therapy. Through a linguistic analysis, she points out the unidirectionality of terms used to describe events in the therapy encounter, indicating very little activity on the part of the client. Here again, therapist behaviour alone is considered, and the client is assumed to have no influence on the relationship: power is assumed to be possessed by the therapist alone, and exerted over a powerless client.

Mystification

Another aspect of the powerful position of the therapist is demonstrated by the mystification of therapy. Pilgrim asserts that 'Mystification and invalidation victimise the patient' (1983, p. 130). False authority can be set up for therapists through mystification of their activity, and Spinelli (1998) suggests that, for therapists to regain any authority that they deserve, they first need to give up the false authority of professionalism and mystification. He refers to the media's portrayal of therapists as dangerous, charlatans or jesters, and contends that

> While that's unfair I think to some extent therapists have a responsibility for it by their unwillingness to talk openly about what it is that we do and the limitations of what we can offer people. We need to be ordinary and admit the lack of knowledge which is at the heart of any deep human encounter.

Here Spinelli seems to allow more for a relationship in which both parties participate. By referring specifically to the notion of authority rather than an undefined notion of power, he allows for the fact that the power of the therapist is determined by whether the client recognises their authority; here clients have more agency than powerless passive victims.

These critiques begin to point to the relationship between power and knowledge, indicating how the possession of legitimised knowledge gives power. However, it is assumed that the therapist (who has the legitimised knowledge about defining the client's problems) holds power, and that the power is unidirectional and oppressive. In most cases, clients are again assumed to be passive victims of power.

Consequences of the power imbalance

The effect on the therapist

It is argued that the effects of the power imbalance in therapy are to increase this imbalance even further. Kipnis's (1976) examination of powerholders and the metamorphic effects of power can be applied to the effects for therapists of being in a position of power. The model used assumes, again, that one person holds power over another who is powerless; thus, it is unidirectional. It also becomes clear that the exercise of power is assumed to be negative, which is then justified later by the conclusions concerning the effects of the exercise of power. First, Kipnis points out that powerholders hold themselves back from scrutiny, which fits with the mystification of therapy by therapists. In a review of empirical studies, he looks at the different strategies used by powerholders in different contexts and the results of these strategies. He then examines the metamorphic effects of power; the changes in the powerholders' conception of themselves and of the target of influence when power is used by the powerholder and is relatively unchallenged over a period of time. He notes that the powerholders' belief in their own worth increases with successful influence of others, and at the same time powerholders devalue the worth of those less powerful and increase their distance from them.

From this model it would follow that, the more therapists successfully influence clients, the more they believe that they know best, the less they think of their clients, and the more they distance themselves from them. These consequences are notably opposite to the way for a therapist to be effective as suggested by 40 years of psychotherapy research. Bozarth (1998) demonstrates how research, time and time again, points to the importance of a warm understanding therapeutic relationship. Kipnis's study points to the importance of a person's internal attitudes concerning the operations of power, although the focus of study is only how the use of power affects internal attitudes, and the reverse (how internal attitudes may affect the use of power) is not considered. Again, this model also assumes that the power of the therapist goes unchallenged and assumes no resistance or agency on the part of the client.

The effect on the client

The effect on the client of the therapist's power is also documented and is argued to be anti-therapeutic. Spinelli (1998) describes a possible consequence of the therapist's assumed expertise and accorded power when he suggests that, by the therapist directing the conversation, the conversation is stilted and the client ends up feeling unheard and coerced into accepting the therapist's ideas, even if they make no sense to the client. Here, Spinelli is assuming that the exercise of power by the therapist is necessarily oppressive and that power is unidirectional from the therapist, who is powerful, to the client, who is powerless. Similarly, Rowe warns against the dangerous effects of therapists believing they know what is best for their clients and 'denying other people's truths'. She cautions: 'Whenever our truth is denied, ignored or invalidated we experience the greatest fear we can ever know: the threat of the annihilation of our self' (1989, p. 17).

Again, the concept of power is one that is assumed to be negative and unproductive. Similarly, the therapist is the one who possesses power and the client is assumed to be powerless; power is conceived as static and monolithic. Moreover, various models of therapy are undifferentiated, and the possibility of a different model of therapy, where the therapist does not believe they know what is best for clients, or want to direct therapy, is not considered.

Social control

Many authors have put forward the idea that therapy serves the function of social control, and that this is based on the use of the power and authority given to the therapist. In this case, parallels between the power structures in society and the structures of power between therapist and client are drawn. Pilgrim (1983) argues that doctors wield control and power in the health service, and illness is theorised using a very inadequate medical model. However, despite the inadequacies of explanation inherent in the medical model, particularly in mental illness, it serves a function of social control by individualising society's sickness and diagnosing it to be treatable by the medical profession. He notes that in an improved society distress will still be there, but that it is historically recent to call this distress 'illness' and give medicine power over individuals with distress, to describe and treat. He suggests that psychotherapies offer some liberation from the medical model, but the extent of this liberation is dependent on the awareness of the social context by the particular model of therapy in question. Here, Pilgrim's social control model of power is structural: power is monolithic, held by the institutions and wielded over powerless individuals in an oppressive way. However, in his later writing (for example in Pilgrim, 1997), he appears to have been more influenced by concepts of power following Foucault.

Hurvitz (1973) too drew the conclusion that psychotherapy is a means of social control, by pointing to the lack of evidence for the effectiveness of psychodynamic psychotherapy and yet the persistence of this therapy in America. He suggests that

> psychodynamic psychotherapy, which is in accord with the individualistic and competitive social mobility system and the ideology of liberal democracy of American capitalism, has a latent purpose that is more important than its manifest purpose; and this latent purpose is to serve as a means of social control. This is accomplished through the ideology and practice of psychotherapy. (Hurvitz, 1973, p. 233)

Clearly, here again, the focus is on the state possessing power over its subjects, using a structural model of power.

Hurvitz elucidates a further consequence of therapy serving the purpose of social control with respect to the ideology of individualising. He explains:

> Psychotherapy is thus based on and fosters an ideology that accepts the status quo and its institutions, and it proposes that changing individuals is the way to change society. (p. 233)

In addition, Hurvitz points out that 'Psychotherapy creates powerful support for the established order — it challenges, labels, manipulates, rejects or co-opts those who attempt to change society' (p. 237). Adcock and Newbigging further explain the connection between social control and scientificism:

> Psychology thus becomes impervious to any body of knowledge that is critical unless that knowledge adheres to the 'science' rules, which in turn function to support prevailing power relations. (1990, p. 174)

The literature concerning psychology or therapy and social control seems to be based on a mixture of models of power. The concern with social control is based to some extent on a monolithic, structural notion of power held by institutions and government over its subjects who are powerless. Within the discussions about social control, it seems to be conceived as always negative and oppressive, although there seems to be more concern with strategies of power and ways of legitimising power, including the use of science. However, in the discussions of social control, the people upon whom this control is seen to be exercised (i.e. clients) are treated very much as 'docile bodies', as passive victims of this power; there is no notion of resistance.

Social structural positions of power (*Societal Power*)

Correlation of structural positions with distress

There is a strong political argument that psychology and therapy individualise distress and thus conceal societal problems. Fundamental to this argument is the idea that society is structured in such a way that different groups of people are endowed with differing levels of power or powerlessness. The assumption is usually made that these structures are fixed and individuals' positions determined and stable, to the extent that their identities can be determined. It is also assumed that each person in a certain position in the structure will be endowed with an equal amount of power. For example, all men have more power, and oppress all women. Here again, the concept of power is of power as a possession, and is unidirectional (for example, the idea that middle-class people have power over working-class people, that men have power over women, etc.) The structures are based on dualisms, with one group assumed to possess power (such as white people) and the other group (such as black people) to be powerless. However, these ideas have been developed in response to criticisms about the omission of the agency of individuals. Structural positions are now more generally understood to create multiple and shifting identities.

There is evidence that the causes of psychological distress are, at least in part, in the structure of society, and that the prevalence of psychological distress is related to the structural positions of individuals in society. Income differences are crucially important determinants of the subjective quality of life among populations (Bostock, 1998). Bostock also notes that

> Those people with most demands and limited resources, such as the physically disabled, the unemployed, carers, single people and poorer social class groups are more likely to be at risk of significant psychological suffering. (1998, p. 2)

Social scientists have documented social causes and correlates for psychological distress, such as Brown and Harris (1978), who identified social risk factors for depression that included unemployment, and being a single mother — particularly with several young children and little support. Lack of social structural power has been argued to be a cause of depression. Gilbert (1992) provides evidence of this from ranking theory and suggests that 'there are biological similarities between low rank status and depression'. He notes evidence to suggest that the prevalence of depression is higher among groups of lower-rank status, and questions whether therapy can help people with depression to increase their power, given the powerlessness inherent for the client in the therapeutic situation. The causal link between powerlessness and psychological distress adds further weight to the critique of the detrimental effects of the structurally powerless position of the client in therapy.

Feminist critiques of psychology and therapy have focused on the omission of the socio-political context and structures of power in society. Adcock and Newbigging (1990) argue that lack of attention to the social context in clinical psychology is the result of individualism and scientificism, the claim for psychological models to be scientific, objective and value-free. 'This we now see as the very processes by which science, as an instrument of patriarchy and capitalism, treats and dismisses women's experiences' (p. 173). The effects of this scientificism is to promote the power and status of therapists, while ignoring or exacerbating the oppression that is the result of the social structures of power (Ussher, 1990; Clements and Rapley, 1996; Haworth, 1998). Further, the exclusion of the socio-political context in therapy serves to maintain the system that produced the individuals who are needing help, thereby perpetuating the social causes of psychological distress (O'Reilly, 1983). Therapists could easily be accused of being self-serving by perpetuating a system that creates the clients who come to see them and maintains the institution of therapy.

Relevance of structural positions to behaviour of therapist and client

The evidence is well documented showing the inequality of the social structural positions between therapists and clients (e.g. Garrett and Davis, 1995; Binnett et al., 1995). Therapists are more likely to be white and middle class, whereas clients are generally poorer, more disabled mentally and physically, older, younger, more dependent and less socially supported. These differences are particularly in evidence for therapists working with clients as part of the NHS, in the UK. In addition, there is much evidence demonstrating the over-representation of individuals from oppressed groups within the mental health system, particularly women and people having African or Caribbean ethnic origins (e.g. Pilgrim, 1997; Williams and Watson, 1994). So it is likely that there will be other aspects of inequality with respect to the social structural positions of therapist and client, with therapists more likely to be in more powerful structural positions. The other side of this is that people from oppressed groups who become therapists may take on characteristics of the mainstream group in order to survive and 'pass' (see Goffman, 1963). For example, working-class therapists may hide their class background and appear to be middle-class, and therapists from ethnic minorities may behave and appear 'white'. The relevance of the socio-political context to therapy and implications for training is documented by Attenborough et al. (2000).

There is evidence that the way therapists use the power inherent in their role is dependent on their structural positions in society. Cooke and Kipnis (1986) found that the use of power varies depending on the gender of the powerholder (the therapist) and the gender of the target (the client). Here, within the terminology, it is apparent that the concept of power is of one person holding power (the powerholder) over another (the target, or passive victim). This is an example of a structural concept of power described in Chapter 3. They found that female therapists interrupted their client 2% of the time compared with male therapists, who interrupted 12% of the time, and in fact that male therapists used all influence tactics (defined as any attempt to change the client) significantly more than female therapists. In addition, therapists of both genders used stronger tactics with female clients than with male clients. For example, they found that female clients were more likely to be told what to do and male clients were more likely to be given explanations. Thus, it seems that an important dimension in the use of power by therapists is the gender of both the therapist and client, and perhaps also other aspects of the identities of both.

In addition, individual therapists varied in their use of influence tactics, demonstrating that there are also individual factors in how powerholders use their power. Perhaps there is a suggestion here that internal attitudes towards power influence individuals' use of power. This suggests that structural power (in terms of structural positions in society and the power attached to the positions of therapist and client) do not entirely explain the power dynamic in therapy; there are other individual factors at work, which are not completely determined by structures. Being a man is not the only relevant factor about a therapist and how much he will try and influence his client: his internal attitude towards his position and towards power also affects the dynamics of power in the therapy relationship. This begins to describe the complex interrelation of different aspects of power. This is some recognition of the agency of individuals, a challenge to the notion of 'docile bodies', of individuals as passive victims oppressed by power (Butler, 1997).

Responding to the socio-political context

There are wide ranges of responses to the accusation that therapy excludes the socio-political context. Some suggest ways that this can be included within models of therapy, while others are more pessimistic about such a possibility. However, many of these arguments are rife with various definitions of power and a failure to distinguish between different aspects of power.

Incompatibility of politics and psychology?
Some argue that this inclusion is impossible, because the goals of politics and psychology are incompatible. The main thesis of Kitzinger and Perkins' (1993) critique of psychology from the perspective of lesbian feminism is that psychology individualises distress caused by oppression and prohibits societal change and community and is therefore dangerous to the goals of feminism. Their main point is that they believe problems should be dealt with from a political rather than a psychological perspective. They suggest that psychology has transformed language and understanding

from the political realm to the individual psychological realm. Psychology has reformulated the notion of power, from an external, political, structural, societal notion to an internal one — as they describe it, 'an awareness, an affirmation, a belief that you already have power, albeit power that the culture does not recognise' (p. 42). To clarify their distinction between these two forms of power, they assert:

> 'Empowerment' then means redefining the word 'power' in such a way that we get to feel we've got some of it. It attempts to create women in a certain state of mind . . . while leaving structural conditions unchanged. (p. 44)

The external 'power' that they want to address they define as follows:

> Lesbians and feminists say that we want power. By 'power' we mean economic power, the power to prevent male violence against women, power to speak and be heard, power to define our own experience of the world, in our own terms. (p. 48)

In contrast, they define psychological 'power', saying

> Psychology redefines 'power' as ours already, waiting to be tapped. 'Power' in psychological language, is a sense of personal agency quite unrelated to the objective and material facts of our lives. Psychology has redefined 'power' in privatised and individualised terms antithetical to radical lesbian politics.

Here they are referring to three distinct concepts of power. First, they argue that women do not have structural material power, from a feminist structural perspective, because men are the sole possessors of this power. This model of power is a classic structural concept of power as monolithic, unidirectional and oppressive. Second, they argue that they want power, and they describe a power that has more in common with Arendt's concept of empowerment, or the feminist concept of '*power-with*' — a power over one's own life, not over anyone else, but a power to influence and be listened to by others. They then refer to psychology's concept of power, which they describe as an internal, personal concept of power, unrelated to structures of society, which is related to the feminist concept of '*power-from-within*'. They go on to dismiss completely any notion of '*power-from-within*', suggesting that an individual's position with respect to power is determined by nothing more than their fixed structural position, thus invoking the notion of passive victims of power, subjects with no agency. They claim that the only valid conception of power is the political structural concept of '*power-over*', which they use as a very stable, fixed and essentialist notion, and they dismiss as unimportant the differences in personal internal power among people who have the same level of structural power. This is a view of structural determinism in which there is no room for the agency of individuals; it fails to explain feminist activism (among other things), as there is no notion of resistance to structures in their understanding of power. I argue that their position, of structural determinism, misses the complex interactions among all these forms of power.

Psychology and 'internal' power, or 'power-from-within'

Others criticise psychology for its focus on internal power and its ignoring of social structural power. Pilgrim states that psychology has concentrated on the notion of internal power and has undervalued the notion of structural power; psychology 'has been hijacked by individualism, so that social change is judged irrelevant, dangerous or a poor substitute for a more valuable change of heart' (1983, p. 127). Smail (1995) usefully provides some clarity about the distinction between internal and structural power. He claims the importance and pervasiveness of power, saying:

> Power is in fact the medium of our social existence, the dynamic which moves the apparatus of our relations with each other . . . It is the power of others which either hurts or supports us, our own power which enables us to establish an at least precarious perch from which to survey and deal with the world. (p. 348)

Here Smail points to the futility of trying to avoid the use of power; he also implies possible benefits of power when he suggests that the power of others can support us and that our own sense of internal power sustains us.

Smail's concept of power is moving away from a unitary, monolithic concept of power to suggest that power is everywhere, and in the dynamics in any relationship. In saying that the power of others can support us, he seems to be suggesting a notion of power, derived from Arendt, that collectivity can increase power, which also fits with the feminist notion of '*power-with*'. He also seems to be following Foucault with his assertion that power is ubiquitous and can be positive.

However, Smail then continues to concur with Kitzinger and Perkins (1993) by explicitly dismissing internal power as a valid concept. He contends:

> Power, including that available to the individual for, so to speak, his/her personal use, is external and material, not internal and spiritual. It is something we acquire from outside, not something we find within ourselves. (Smail, 1995, p. 351)

He asserts that psychology usually concerns itself with internal 'power' or 'will power', and talk of 'empowerment' 'by forms of psychological exhortation or manipulation which will somehow encourage them to tap supposed internal resources of optimism and determination (will power in some disguise or other)'. He thus describes the 'slide into the "psychologizing" of power as an internal, personal attribute'.

Here, Smail emphasises the importance of power as a notion that is relational, not a possession that someone has internally. However, he is not convinced that internal attitudes or a feeling of internal agency have any relevance to the use or abuse of power. This view fails to explain the variation in people's positions of power who have the same structural identities, and fails to take account of the way power is internalised and constitutes the psyche (Butler, 1997; and see Chapter 4).

Psychology and structural power
Some authors suggest psychology should be much more concerned with the structural positions and material realities of peoples' lives with respect to power. Smail is concerned only with structural power and implores psychology to take account of the reality of external power, which is a real factor in the aetiology of psychological distress and therefore, he contends, must be a factor in the amelioration of the distress. He proposes a broader than internal individual psychology, criticising the individualism of psychology: 'I think this is a profound mistake and disconnects psychology from a tradition which considered the psyche as the product of social and environmental influences' (1995, p. 354). Also voting for inclusion of the environment within psychology, Bostock (1998) suggests that

> Recognising wider social and environmental influences on people's psychological functioning enriches therapeutic formulations, addresses criticisms of formal therapies lacking applicability to groups other than the white middle class.

Smail points out that, if clinical psychology addresses issues of external power,

> We shall arrive at a more realistic understanding of what is therapeutically possible once it becomes clear to us that neither we nor our clients have unlimited access to power, indeed often have no access at all to control over the kinds of powers which so often shape our characters and damage our relations with each other. (p. 355)

He promotes a different idea of what therapy should involve from this perspective:

> Clinical practice with individuals, from this point of view, becomes a process involving both the analysis of power and the provision of support-through-solidarity . . . It might clarify things quite a lot to view the therapeutic relationship as in itself the provision of a form (albeit limited) of power.

Smail further advocates that we need to think about how to use whatever power we have positively, to increase the power of others, to take care, to enlighten, to love rather than exploit, and in general to think seriously about the obligations as opposed to the advantages of power.

Here, Smail seems to suggest that, through the therapy relationship, people can be given power, or perhaps can gain power through association with a more powerful person, or even just through solidarity with another. This concept seems to be derived from Arendt's concept of power and the feminist notion of '*power-with*', a different aspect of power from the structural power that is his usual preoccupation. With the suggestion of working to increase structural power in therapy, he opens up the notion of structural power being less fixed and deterministic, leaving more room for individuals to have agency within their social context. However, in an effort to redress the balance with respect to psychology's ignoring of the social context, he seems to discard any notions of effects on the psyche of more micro-level relations with others. He begins to extend the notion of structural power to admitting the possibility of positive uses of '*power-with*', but then stays with a concept of power solely determined by structural positions.

Summary and conclusion

I have examined the literature on power in therapy. First, the critique of the inequality in the roles of therapist and client was examined. In much of this literature, this power is treated as a possession of the therapist, with the client assumed to be powerless and denied agency. There also seems to be the implicit assumption that relationships without dynamics of power are possible. Sometimes this aspect of power is confused with other aspects, but mostly power is treated as a possession, unfairly held by the therapist and wielded over the client in an oppressive way. Little consideration is given to models of therapy, particularly person-centred therapy, where the power inherent in the role of the therapist is challenged.

Other literature focuses on the avoidance within psychology and therapy of the socio-political context and structural positions of power. Within this literature, this aspect of power is generally considered as the only form of power to be considered, and psychology is criticised for its focus on more 'internal' aspects of power. Some authors conclude that therapists should take social structural aspects of power into account, whereas others conclude that therapy is incompatible with a political analysis of structural aspects of power. Again, power is treated as a possession, held by some and wielded over others, subjects with no agency. More dynamic and intra-psychic aspects of power are ignored or deemed irrelevant.

In all the literature examined, no writers explore the dynamic relationship between the therapist and client from the perspective of both parties. The therapist is assumed to possess power and the client to be powerless, a 'docile body' with no agency, upon whom power is inflicted. There is no notion of resistance and very little notion of how the personal histories of the individuals may affect the relationship. The therapy relationship is treated very much as a static thing, determined only by the structural positions of the individuals. The power possessed by the therapist is seen as negative, and it is implied that the least power possessed by the therapist over the client, the better.

This literature has been useful for raising the awareness of therapists concerning structural aspects of power both in the role of the therapist and in the social structure of society. However, it has missed the opportunity to consider the complex interactions of various aspects of power, including more dynamic and intra-psychic forms. The focus on power as a possession misses the dynamic and relational nature of power and this structural determinism leaves little option to work with dynamics of power in a positive way.

Chapter 3

What is power? Structural theories

Aim of this chapter

This chapter briefly describes the theoretical and historical basis of structural theories of power. These are theories that describe structures of power, assuming that power is a possession and is held by a person or group of people over others in a negative way. These structural theories lie within the context of Modernism, a period of history of knowledge following the Enlightenment and Romantic periods, which has dominated most of the twentieth century. Concepts fundamental to modernist theories are the belief in science as representing truth, in language as representing the truth about the world and dualistic thinking (such as man/woman; body/mind, etc.). Post-modernism challenged these assumptions and ways of looking at the world and knowledge, and, within post-modernism, post-structuralism similarly challenged structures of the world and knowledge. Chapter 4 describes poststructural theories of power.

The relevance of structural theories to the therapy relationship is limited, with a causal and mechanistic view of power limiting the understanding of power in a dynamic relationship between two people. These limits are described by Clegg:

> The questions posed within the 'foundational' tradition of power in its modernity . . . can be understood as so many ritual moves through the rules of a particular language game which has become thoroughly restrictive. (1989, p. 37)

Further, Clegg contends that the questions posed within the structural definitions of power are framed 'as if a conceptual arachnid were endlessly weaving a linguistic funnel-web within which to ensnare our understanding' (1989, p. 37). Using structural theories alone leads to structural determinism, where people are determined by their positions and to the notion of people being victims of their circumstances, with no agency.

However, structural theories of power remind us of the pervasive patterns of power that do structure our lives and provide a context for every individual. These are necessary to consider in therapy, particularly with respect to the relevance of people in structurally powerless positions, where psychological distress is a direct result of such positions. In addition, the positions of therapist and client are placed within the context of a structure of power where the therapist has authority and power over the client. Structural models of power help us to understand how these structures within which we all live impact on the therapy relationship.

I hope to be able to describe the foundations for modernist conceptions of power and to demonstrate how common understandings of power have led to certain questions and ways of investigating and understanding power. At the same time, the aim is to point out the limitations of these questions, and in later chapters to investigate models and concepts of power beyond Clegg's modernist 'linguistic funnel-web'. These alternative models of power are derived, in the main, from a Machiavellian notion of power.

The foundation of theories of power: Hobbes and Machiavelli

The first theorists to describe and analyse frameworks of power from an analytic rather than an ethical or religious stance were Machiavelli (in the sixteenth century) and Hobbes (in the seventeenth century). Hobbes's and Machiavelli's contributions to concepts of power provided the basis for two competing ways of speaking about power: a discursive tension, which was resolved in favour of Hobbes's modernist theory rather than that of Machiavelli (Clegg, 1989).

Hobbes

Hobbes's concept of power formed the basis for modernist and structural thinking about power and thus has shaped our understanding and experience of the modern world. This model is described by Clegg as 'a view of power initiated by human agency, expressed through causal relations and measurable in terms of mechanistic indicators' (1989, p. 22). Power is seen mechanically and behaviourally; A has power over B, say, when A causes B to do something. For example, the therapist has power over the client when the therapist persuades a client who self-injures to try and talk about their feelings instead of cutting. All structural theories that followed used this model of power, viewing power as a possession, and as monolithic and unitary (held in one place and having one form) and unidirectional (held by one group of people). With this model, power was also necessarily conceived of as negative and oppressive. This concept of power was used to describe control by a certain group of people, for example the state (in theories of democracy), men (in feminist theories of patriarchy) or the ruling class (in Marxist theories). It forms the basis for what is regarded as the central tradition of inquiry into power. In most of the literature on power and therapy this model of power is used, where the therapist holds structural power over the client and where this is necessarily negative.

Machiavelli

In contrast, the Machiavellian concept of power was about strategic manoeuvres. Machiavelli conceived of power as dissonant with no overall harmonic, i.e. occurring in many directions in many forms and with no central guiding or organising principle. So, for example, on a psychiatric ward, an analysis of power following Machiavelli would not investigate how the staff have power over the clients (as a structural analysis would), but instead would explore the dynamics of power in all relationships and the strategies that each individual uses to influence others. Machiavelli insisted on studying strategies of power wherever and whatever they might be, rather than being restricted by any a priori mechanical or causal conceptions. He had no moral stance towards power but merely described where he found it. For Machiavelli,

> Power is simply the effectiveness of strategies for achieving for oneself a greater scope for action than for others implicated by one's strategies. Power is not anything nor is it necessarily inherent in any one; it is a tenuously produced and reproduced effect which is contingent upon the strategic competencies and skills of actors who would be powerful . . . It is this stress on description, on interpretation, on the translation of power, that signals Machiavelli's distinctiveness . . . It is in the very prosaic refusal of any grand theory or meta-narrative, above all, that Machiavelli's distinctiveness resides. (Clegg, 1989, p. 32)

Thus, for Machiavelli, there was no restriction as to who could wield power, and his main question was how this power was wielded, what strategies were used. There was no conception of a unitary monolithic power, but rather one of dissonant strategies of power used by different individuals or groups of people. Using this model of power in therapy, it would not be assumed that only the therapist held power over the client; the way the therapist and the client influence each other and the strategies they both use would be investigated.

Theories of state power

Hobbes and Weber

Hobbes's mechanistic view of power underlies the current strength of the view of power as a causal relation, and a relatively unified state power. Hobbes believed in loyalty to a monarch as a moral principle. He suggested that power and cause are the same thing; thus, power was expressed in terms of motion. In Hobbes's model, power can be negative only, because people cannot have agency: what they can choose from is already chosen. For example, in therapy a client can choose only between which models of therapy are chosen to be provided by the therapists. For Hobbes, the state determines which voices are legitimised according to the rules of science and rationality. Again, a parallel in the provision of therapy would be the current use of 'evidence-based practice' to determine which therapies should be provided. Hobbes adopted a moral stance in his chosen role as legislator, aiming to design the right method for constituting power. He stressed the legitimate identification with respect to science of the means of power, and the concern for good order in the end that power serves; i.e. he believed that power was justified by the appeal to science and rationality that should guide the movements of the people.

Weber's model of political power followed the Hobbesian tradition of the structural notion of power.[1] He saw bureaucracy (the organisation of government by committees and officials and hierarchical levels of decision-making) as occupying a central place within the historical processes of modernisation, being inseparably linked to the development of the territorial state and the capitalist economy. Here, links can be made to the bureaucratic organisation of the NHS and the way decisions (most obviously about the prescription of medication) are linked to the global capitalist economy. At the time Weber was writing, the administration of government had been opened (from those with inherited wealth, i.e. the aristocracy) to those with access to education, thus opening up a limited form of democracy. He also linked this to bureaucracy. He saw bureaucracy as being underpinned by a more scientific approach to knowledge rather than tradition (reflecting the change from an aristocratic elite to an intellectual elite), to impose order on the world rather than adjust to it.

In concordance with power necessarily being negative and oppressive, Weber also saw bureaucracy as a threat to the values of the liberal non-bureaucratic elite — the values of individual freedom and the scope for exceptional individuals to play a role in the economy and the state. He was concerned by the threat to individual freedom; how was it going to be possible to preserve any element of independent thought or action in the face of organisational structures that constrained the individual by their discipline on members, and through their wider social

---

1. However, Weber was concerned to preserve the tension between individual agency and structures of power. He was not a structural determinist. He was also influenced by Nietzsche.

power? He was worried that this would lead to a society of security and precise regulation rather than innovative risk-taking approaches. Again, it could be argued that the current climate of 'evidence-based practice' in the NHS similarly constrains innovative and creative ways of working for therapists working in this system. Weber is quoted in Beetham as saying:

> The central question is what we can oppose to this machinery, in order to keep a portion of humanity free from this pigeon-holing of the spirit, from the total domination of the bureaucratic ideal. (Beetham, 1996, p. 55)

While he saw increasing levels of bureaucracy as inevitable, Weber's ideal solution was control of the bureaucracy from above by an elite (i.e. by those whose individual freedom he was concerned to preserve). But he also suggested the need to find something to counterpose bureaucracy, believing that by creating a balance of social forces individual freedom could be secured in the tension between them. Weber's theory of power demonstrates the necessarily negative and repressive concept of power underpinning the structural concept of power.

Both Hobbes's and Weber's theories of power also demonstrate the value placed on science that is characteristic of the Enlightenment period and modernist/structuralist theories (see Fig. 3a). This reliance on the universal rationality of science was only later brought into question by feminist and post-structuralist theories demonstrating the relationship between power and knowledge. These theories of power can be particularly identified in the principles and philosophy behind cognitive-behaviour therapy, where science is used to justify the expert position of the therapist.

Fig. 3a
Theories of state power

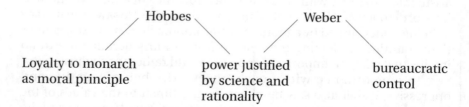

Marxism and Gramsci's theory of hegemony

The Marxist approach is to locate bureaucracy within a wider theory of class domination and class conflict. Marxist theory sees both bureaucracy and the elite as part of class domination, and the solution as a revolution culminating in a post-class society with democratic control from below. Marx contended that the state cannot represent the public as a whole. Classes have fundamental differences of interest, and these differences largely define economic and political life. The state privileges those with property and defends private ownership and the means of production. Marx described the repressive functions of the state as an information network for surveillance, and one with the capacity to sustain the belief in the inviolability of existing arrangements, i.e. to convince the public of the impossibility of change. Again, in Marxist theory the trademarks of the structural approach to power are clear — the necessarily negative concept of power as a monolithic possession, which is unidirectional. The upper classes hold power over the working classes. The Marxist concept of 'alienation' (the result for the workers of state control of production — alienation from the process and products of labour, and from other workers) provides a theory to explain one way in which psychological distress is caused by class positions and the powerlessness of the working classes.

Gramsci extended Marxist ideas of revolution and power by extending the concept of hegemony (see Fig. 3b). He used the concept of hegemony to explain the conditions necessary for the successful overthrow of one social class by another. He said that this depended on solidarity and leadership. When these conditions are fulfilled, the new social group can be said to be hegemonic. Gramsci uses 'hegemony' to distinguish between the various methods of control available to the dominant social group.[2] He distinguishes between coercive and consensual control. He explains that consensual control arises when individuals 'willingly' assimilate the worldview or hegemony of the dominant group, which allows the group to be hegemonic. He further suggests that all institutions have both a material and an ideational impact on individuals, and that coercion and consent tend to combine. For example, within psychiatry, the Mental Health Act can be used to force individuals to be 'treated'; however, some psychiatric patients also choose to give control to the psychiatric establishment to treat them. Many patients would fall somewhere between these two extremes, with the fear of coercion and pressure from others perhaps influencing them to give 'consent' or, more accurately, to comply with treatment.

Gramsci's concept of hegemony extended the Marxist concept of power to ideology and to the act of constituting individuals by the action on the unconscious and the shaping of interests. However, this concept of power still remains firmly within a structural view of power, preserving the idea of a unified monolithic state power, by invoking the concept of 'false or manipulated consciousness'. Clegg explains:

> It is a way of not taking people seriously; of regarding them as having been culturally duped; of preserving, against contra-indications, a view of power as orchestrated by a single sovereign, ruling entity.

2. For more details on Gramsci's theory of hegemony, see Ransome (1992).

> What makes it seem so may be less the nature of empirical tendencies and more the mythical meta-narratives of a grand and systemic view of the world. (1989, p. 29)

Clegg criticises the view of seeing people as having no agency, as machines to be manipulated. Here his critique of the structural grand theory of power hints at an alternative discontinuous and strategic concept of power for which Machiavelli laid the groundwork. However, the acknowledgement of the relationship between knowledge and beliefs and power and the effects of power in shaping consciousness can be seen as a precursor to Foucault's later extension of the relationship between power, knowledge and ideology. In psychiatry, where the medical model is so well publicised and funded, it is clear that, despite obvious challenges to its validity, the ideology convinces many patients that it is in their best interests to believe they suffer from an 'illness'.

Fig. 3b
Theories of class power

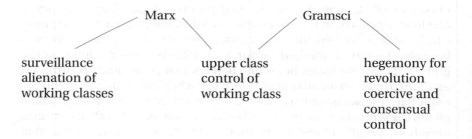

Marx		Gramsci
surveillance	upper class	hegemony for
alienation of	control of	revolution
working classes	working class	coercive and
		consensual
		control

Lukes' dimensions of power

Three dimensions of power were introduced by Lukes (1974) (see Fig. 3c). He advocates the three-dimensional view as superior to the previous conceptions.

The one-dimensional model of power was that of the pluralists, such as Dahl. This concept of power is a purely mechanistic view, following the Hobbesian tradition. According to the pluralists, A has power over B when A influences B to do something he would not otherwise do. The emphasis is on concrete observable decision-making where there is observable conflict of interests, and is applied to political decision-making. For example, within a Department of Health committee, a political figure with shares in a particular pharmaceutical company persuades a psychiatrist to agree to recommend a particular medication for prescription practices for GPs. Within this model, power is a form of compulsion exerted by the (relatively) powerful upon one another within political institutions designed to promote the aims and interests of competing groups. It is of, by and for elites. Within this one-dimensional view, women are construed as apolitical beings by definition. Women are neither the As with power or the Bs being compelled. They are not part of the political arena. Elshtain emphasises: 'Women do not figure in the geometry of power relations' (1992, p. 112).

Critics of the pluralists, for example Bachrach and Boratz, developed the two-dimensional view of power. They claimed that power is demonstrated also in non-decision-making, in the mobilisation of bias that determines what decisions are made and suppresses the possibilities of challenges to the decision-maker. This second dimension redefines the boundaries of what constitutes a political issue, but within this model it is still assumed that power is demonstrated by conflict and that people's interests are consciously articulated and observable. Following the above example, the second dimension is illustrated by the chair of the committee deciding the items for the agenda, and the psychiatrist being prevented from discussing or including anything in the report about alternatives to medication. The second dimension of power widened the scope of what was necessary to consider political, extending the arena of politics to cover private as well as public life, and thus being more inclusive of women's lives. Elshtain explains:

> It disrupted the complacency with which mainstream political scientists justified non-participation in political life by assuring themselves that those who did not participate in politics were those for whom participation was not a value. (1992, p. 113)

Lukes then adds the third dimension of power. He describes political power as a function of collective forces and social arrangements, and says that power is not just demonstrated by conflict between individuals. The third dimension of power involves the determining and shaping of what people want, of what their interests are in the first place. Lukes notes that manipulation and authority are also manifestations of power and that the most effective and insidious use of power prevents conflicts.[3] The third dimension of power, according to Lukes, concerns the latent conflict between the interests of those effecting power and the 'real' interests of those they exclude. Again, following the above example, this dimension would be demonstrated by the 'information' circulated by government bodies, citing particular research 'results' said to demonstrate the efficacy of medication and the dangers of not prescribing such medication. This 'information' is then used by certain groups of service users and carers to argue for increased control and means to increase compliance with medication. The way the government presents 'information' about mental health through the media plays a role in determining what the public want

---

3. The most effective use of power being in the absence of violence is reminiscent of Arendt — see later section.

in terms of mental health care and leads to increased control, justified by 'public pressure' which has first been created by political agendas and the media.

The difficulty of this third dimension lies in knowing how to determine people's 'real' interests, although Lukes suggests that it is possible to try to identify what people would do if they were not under power. He points out that with the three dimensions of power there is a complex interplay between individual motivations and group structural concerns. He notes that, as someone may not be conscious of the exercising of power, it can cause difficulties with the attribution of responsibility. He advocates that a three-dimensional analysis of power relations is possible, but points out that this analysis is of necessity theoretical, empirical and value-laden. Morals must be involved in an analysis of power.

Fig. 3c
Lukes' dimensions of power

1st Dimension	A influences B to make particular decision
2nd Dimension	Decisions to be made are suppressed
3rd Dimension	Shaping people's interests

Lukes further extended the structuralist concept of power by adding the dimension of ideology and the shaping of individuals' consciousness. This extended the structuralist model of power in a similar way to that of Gramsci's concept of hegemony, and perhaps to the limits of this model, paving the way for the alternative post-structuralist models of power based on the foundations of Machiavelli. Smail (1987) refers to the manipulation of interests as described by Lukes and to how powerful a way it is of ordering social relations. He suggests that in this make-believe world, 'What matters is not what is, but what people can be made to believe' (p. 400). Each model of therapy that has an aim to make people think or behave in a certain way could be said to be using Lukes' third dimension of power to manipulate and shape how people see their best interests. Even more openly, in psychiatry patients are led to believe that medication is in their best interests, despite all the dangers and evidence to the contrary (see for example Breggin, 1993).

Arendt's concept of power

Arendt introduced a new idea of power. Rather than the concept of power over people, the oppressive concept of power, she introduced the notion of power by collectivity as a positive means (see Fig. 3d). She used this notion in describing the philosophical basis of the American Constitution, that of power by consent. She explained how, for the people of the American Revolution,

> Power came into being when and where people would get together and bind themselves through promises, covenants, and mutual pledges; only such power, which rested on reciprocity and mutuality, was real power and legitimate, whereas the so-called power of kings or princes or aristocrats, because it did not spring from mutuality, but at best rested on consent, was spurious and usurped. (Arendt, 1963, p. 181)

For Arendt, power is positive, relational and related to freedom. It is about people joining together to increase power for everyone, rather than some people holding power over others. She describes binding, promising and covenanting as the means by which power is retained, and suggests that power disappears when people disperse and desert one another. She talks about the 'enormous potential' (p. 176) of the power in mutuality. Arendt defines power as follows:

> Power corresponds to the human ability not just to act but to act in concert. Power is never the property of an individual; it belongs to a group and remains in existence only so long as the group keeps together. When we say of somebody that he is 'in power' we actually refer to him being empowered by a certain number of people to act in their name. (1986, p. 64)

She contrasts power with strength (a quality of an individual), force (the energy released by physical or social movements), violence and authority (vested in persons or offices such that others obey without coercion or persuasion). She compares power with violence, emphasising that violence is instrumental, whereas power is the condition necessary for any action. She explains: 'Power, far from being a means to an end, is actually the very condition enabling a group of people to think and act in terms of the means-end category' (Arendt, 1986, p. 68).

Arendt's concept of power is clearly a political theory that describes structures of power and government. In this sense, it is a structural theory. However, unlike the modernist tradition of structural theories, she sees power as relational and not necessarily negative. Her notion of power has informed the notion of empowerment in psychiatry and other areas and suggests the positive collective power that can emerge in groups. An example within mental health is the increasing number of non-hierarchical self-help groups. Arendt's distinctions between different terms are also useful in distinguishing particularly between power (in relationships between people) and authority (a possession of an individual held by virtue of a certain role). The concept of people in power being empowered by others gives agency to all individuals and also hints at the concept of resistance to power and authority. Her theory seems to create a bridge between structural and post-structural theories of power.

Feminist theories of power

Feminist theory is the most developed body of theory concerning structural inequalities. Humm describes the various feminist theories and also explains the argument that unites them:

> The emergence of feminist ideas and feminist politics depends on the understanding that, in all societies which divide the sexes into differing cultural, economic or political spheres, women are less valued than men. Feminism also depends on the premise that women can consciously and collectively change their social place.
> (1992, p. 1)

First-wave feminism was concerned principally with equality, and second-wave feminism uses women's differences to oppose the 'rules' of patriarchy.[4] In first-wave feminism women are objects to be given equality, whereas in second-wave feminism women are subjects challenging 'knowledge' from the strength of their own experience. First-wave feminism challenged institutions, whereas second-wave feminism also challenges the invisibility of patriarchy, the more personal sphere of relationships and everyday lives. This represented a move from materialism to the dynamics and psychological aspects of women's lives. The move is paralleled by Lukes' third dimension of the analysis of power, and Gramsci's concept of hegemony with respect to the acknowledgement of the effects of power on the unconscious and the shaping of interests.

Feminist theories of power are based in a structural model of power. Power is seen as monolithic and unitary (held by men), and unidirectional (exerted by men over women). Similarly, power is seen as always negative and oppressive. In response to accusations about feminism excluding many women and treating women as a homogeneous group, some feminist theorists have added other aspects of structure to feminist theory. Socialist feminists add the concept of class to gender — the interaction determining power. Black feminists argue that race, class and gender are interlocking systems of oppression. Feminist theory is useful in theorising and making people aware of the oppression experienced by all oppressed groups, including users of psychiatric services. It also provides useful

---

4. *Patriarchy* is the way society is structured with men holding power. It refers both to concrete systems of power and to the ideology and generally understood attitudes and assumptions that go along with the structures (such as the differing sex-role stereotypes and expectations of men and women).

theories for understanding the relation between oppression and psychological distress. But even taking into consideration all aspects of structural identity, structural feminism has been limited in its ability to predict the dynamic aspects of power between any two people in a relationship.

However, some feminist theorists have extended the notion of power from a purely structural notion. Some psychoanalytic feminists include the notion of personal history and intra-psychic aspects of power. For example, Mitchell has used psychoanalytic theory to explain how the unconscious contributes to gender identity and oppression. Some radical feminists have provided clarity about various concepts of power and moved towards a dynamic post-structural perspective. For French (1985), power is an interaction rather than a substance. She distinguishes between 'power-to' and 'power-over' (p. 505) (see Fig. 3d, over). '*Power-to*' refers to ability, capacity, and connotes a kind of freedom', a sense of the strength of an individual. However, she also notes the relational context, that 'power-to' is achieved by communities supporting individuals, which is reminiscent of Arendt (see above). In contrast, '*power-over*' is domination, coercive authority. Again, however, this is presented as in the context of relationships, not a possession: 'Power is a process, a dynamic interaction . . . One does not possess power; it is granted to the dominator by hosts of other people, and that grant is not unretractable' (p. 509). Here there is a move away from structural determinism towards agency for each person in relationship and the concept of resistance (see explanation of Foucault's work concerning resistance in Chapter 4). She suggests the reappropriation of pleasure, the core of which is mutuality and freedom, as the basis for a new morality beyond power.

Similarly, Starhawk (1987) distinguishes between three types of power: 'power-over', 'power-from-within' and 'power-with' (see Fig. 3d). '*Power-over*' refers to domination, as with French. '*Power-from-within*' comes from the root of the word 'power', meaning to be able, and she describes this as an inner strength from a sense of mastery at one's own ability and innate value. This strength also arises from the sense of connection or bond with other humans and the environment. '*Power-with*' is the power of individuals within a group of equals, to suggest and be listened to. She emphasises the danger that this can become authority and that '*power-with*' is possible only among those who are equal and who recognise they are equal. The usefulness in these distinctions for Starhawk is to provide alternative models of power to domination. She then distinguishes between rebellion and resistance to domination. Whereas rebellion does not change the system, resistance arises from different values to those of domination and affirms the inherent value of individuals.

Starhawk (1987) also explores the intra-psychic effects of power. Whereas feminist theories began firmly within a structural model of power, many feminist theorists have extended theories of power to consider the strategies and intra-psychic effects of relational power and to consider other positive concepts of power as opposed to the negative concept of domination. Starhawk's clarity about the various concepts of power is very useful, and will be used later in this book to apply to power in therapy. The challenge for therapists is to resist using '*power-over*' the client, while not giving up their own '*power-from-within*' and encouraging the client to use their '*power-from-within*'. In addition, it would be useful to work in ways that find opportunities to harness '*power-with*', for example in groups.

Fig. 3d
Aspects of power

Aspects	Theorists	Description
Power-over	State & Class French Starhawk	Domination Coercion Authority
Power-with	Arendt Starhawk	Positive power of collectivity
Power-from-within	Starhawk	Inner strength from sense of own ability and innate value
Power-to	French	Combination of above two: Strength of individual supported by communities

Summary

I have presented various structural theories of power in this chapter. All these models, except Arendt's unique theory of power, have certain characteristics in common: the concept of power is of a certain group holding power (the state in political theories, men in feminist theories of patriarchy, or the ruling class in Marxist theories of capitalism); power is assumed to be unidirectional and power is assumed to be oppressive, necessarily negative. Applying this model to therapy leads to the therapist holding power oppressively over the powerless client. Arendt refers to power as a positive productive concept, and her idea concerns power between people rather than power over people. This is similar to some feminist distinctions between types of power and the positivity of '*power-from-*'

within' and '*power-with'*. I will refer to Arendt's concept of power as a separate theory because of its distinguishing characteristics, and to the other theories presented here as *structural theories*, suggesting the characteristics of power as monolithic, unidirectional, oppressive and a possession.

I argue that structural theories of power remind us of the pervasive structures of power which provide a context for all individuals in society and in therapy (*Societal Power*), and remind us of our responsibilities as citizens to challenge social inequalities. In addition, structural theories are useful to provide a framework for understanding the structural positions of the therapist and the client in these roles (*Role Power*) and the authority invested by society in the role of the therapist. Lukes' three dimensions of power demonstrate how power is involved not only in coercion but also in ideology and the shaping of individuals' best interests. However, I believe that post-structural theories need to be added to structural theories to understand the dynamic aspects of power in the therapy relationship.

Chapter 4

How does power work? Post-structural theories

Introduction

In contrast to structural concepts of power (described in Chapter 3), post-structural concepts focus on different aspects of power. They challenge the implicit assumptions of structural concepts — that power is monolithic, unidirectional and oppressive — and instead present a model of power as ubiquitous. Post-structural models focus on strategies of power, following Machiavelli's concerns. One of the aims of post-structuralists is deconstruction: the unpacking of assumptions and consequences behind theories. A post-structural analysis of power adds a further dimension to Lukes' three dimensions of power (see Chapter 3) by examining how individuals are constituted and positioned by operations of power.

Foucault's discussions of power form the bedrock of post-structuralist work. Nietzsche's model of power provided some of the first concepts used by Foucault and other post-structuralists, particularly the relationship between power and knowledge and the genealogical method.[1] Throughout his work, Foucault is concerned with the analysis of power relations and the techniques of the exercise of power and of the interrelation of power and knowledge. Deleuze and Guattari further developed Foucault's ideas and made the political and ethical value-base clear.

In this chapter, I present Foucault's concept of power in detail, and then consider how this applies to therapy. I go on to explore critiques of Foucault and resolutions of these critiques. I present Deleuze and Guattari's expansion of Foucault's ideas and the contributions of authors applying post-structuralist ideas of deconstruction to power and therapy. These theories demonstrate the theoretical underpinnings of my deconstruction of power in therapy. Post-structuralist theories of power are essential to examine the dynamic relations of power within therapy and to introduce the idea of both the therapist's and the client's agency in

---

1. The genealogical method describes the process of tracing the historical roots and values, the assumptions and the social and political context of a theory or discourse.

the relationship, rather than reducing each to the sum of their structural positions. Finally, I suggest some ways to synthesise structural and post-structural ideas.

Foucault's concept of power

Foucault's consideration of power follows concepts used by Nietzsche. Nietzsche drew attention to the fact that knowledge and thought, theories and discourses[2] are permeated by values (Daudi, 1986). This paved the way for the genealogical approach to analysis; the tracing of the historical roots and values, the historical and political context of a theory. This approach was later adopted by Foucault and formed the basis of his work. Similarly, Nietzsche's idea of the will to truth permeated Foucault's work.[3] However, in contrast to Foucault, Nietzsche's concept of power seems to be also concerned with the intention of the agent of power; the focus is on the 'why?' of power in addition to the 'how?' described by Foucault. Rather than following the Hobbesian tradition of power as described in Chapter 3, Foucault's concern with strategies follows Machiavelli's concerns, and Clegg (1989) suggests that Foucault was also influenced by Gramsci's theory of hegemony (see Chapter 3).

A great proportion of Foucault's works is relevant to the issue of power in the therapeutic relationship. This is because, in addition to addressing the issue of power directly throughout his treatises, and specifically in many articles, lectures and interviews which have been collected in *Power and Knowledge* (1980), Foucault specifically considered the history of madness (*Madness and Civilisation*, 1977) with reference to power. This provides a context for the emergence of the association of the experience of distress and behaviour outside social norms with medicine and social control. He also wrote about the history of sexuality, paying particular attention to the conditions of emergence of psychoanalysis and the psychoanalytic therapeutic relationship (*The History of Sexuality*, Vol. 1, 1981). This theorises the emergence of the context of 'confession' from which the idea of therapy arose. *Discipline and Punish* (1977) was also concerned primarily with his concept of 'disciplinary power'. This concept

---

2. *Discourse* is a central term used in post-structuralist theory. Language, far from *reflecting* an already given social reality, *constitutes* social reality for us, reflecting the site of a political struggle. A discourse is a systematic way of speaking or writing which forms the objects of which it speaks and gives meaning to the world. It emphasises the social and political construction of 'reality' through language and action (see Lowe, 1999). Discourses are a structuring principle of society in social institutions, modes of thought and individual subjectivity.
3. Nietzsche described the 'will to power' as the one basic drive of living creatures. His concept of power was of power over others (domination) and over oneself (ultimately leading to asceticism). He emphasised that values are the voice of the will to power. He asked under what conditions the value judgements of good and evil derived, and from this the genealogical method was developed (see Nietzsche, 1969 and 1977 edns).

followed structural ideas of power more closely (see Chapter 3), examining the techniques by which those in power controlled those subject to this power. Later, Foucault moved away from this concept to focus more on resistance to power and the internalisation of regulatory power by individuals.

(a) Power

Despite the extent of Foucault's consideration of power, he offers no general theory of power. He contends that the question 'What is power?' leads to a misguided analysis of power. Instead, he provides general protocols for the analysis of power relations, more a toolkit for analysis than a general theory, which he terms an 'analytic of relations of power' (*Power and Knowledge*, 1980, p. 199). In not answering the question 'What is power?' Foucault wants to avoid a definition that lays down the nature of power relations in general, the sources and aims behind them and the way in which they are exercised. This analysis for Foucault would not account for a number of phenomena that fall in the domain of power relations; furthermore, he contends that 'power in the substantive sense, le pouvoir, does not exist' (*Power and Knowledge*, 1980, p. 198). Here he is suggesting that power is not a possession that some have and others do not have. His thesis is that relations of power are exercised from innumerable points, are not limited to one domain, take a wide variety of forms and are only partly co-ordinated. For example, within the context of the NHS, it is possible to identify numerable relations of power — between the government and health purchasing bodies, between health purchasers and providers, between consultants and managers, between all different groups of professionals, and of course between service providers and service users. An analysis of these relations of power following Foucault would not assume that all these dynamics arise from the same point or have the same form. Although they all interrelate in some way, it would not be assumed they are co-ordinated in any way.

Foucault is concerned, in his analyses, to ask and answer the question 'By what means is power exercised in specific domains under particular historical conditions?' For Foucault, there is nothing more to power relations than their exercise. Contrary to other analyses of power, for him power relations are examined through the observation and analysis of conduct or action, not through the mind or consciousness. In some ways, Foucault's emphasis on the exercise of power relations is similar to the emphasis of behavioural social scientists (see Chapter 3 and Lukes' first and second dimensions of power); but, unlike previous behaviourist theories, Foucault generally broadens his associations of the exercise of power beyond situations of conflict. So, 'Power means relations, a more-or-less organised, hierarchical co-ordinated cluster of relations' (*Power and Knowledge*, 1980, p. 198). Cousins and Hussein further explain: 'Power denotes the ensemble of actions exercised by and bearing on individuals which guide conduct and structure its possible outcomes' (1984, p. 229).

Foucault critiques previous theories of power, particularly what he terms the 'juridico-discursive' conception of power. This is synonymous with the structural/modernist theories of power described in Chapter 3. These theories describe power held by a certain group or individual over another, power being unidirectional and oppressive. In this conception of a system of power, the exercise of power has the same general form at all levels and in all domains, i.e. that of prohibition or repression. This conception of power asks the questions 'Who holds power?' and 'Who is subject to it?' Foucault, however, denies this all-encompassing division between the 'rulers' and the 'ruled', and contends that the interconnections between local relations of power are established through strategies of power, not through pre-established divisions. Clegg (1989) explains that Foucault attempts to break the mechanistic sovereignty view of power described in Chapter 3; instead, he is concerned with power *within* the social body rather than *from above* it. He uses biological metaphors to describe the local circulation of power, e.g. describing a 'capillary form' of power, a 'synaptic regime of power', to emphasise his focus on particular local relations of power rather than general theory. Foucault emphasises the heterogeneity of power relations, the variety of forms of power relations rather than a general theory. Attention is paid to political aims, strategic objectives, links between aims and objectives, tactics employed by adversaries and the balance of forces. The arenas of struggle are diverse, and so are the forces and their objectives.

Foucault is concerned to analyse the detail of local power relations, 'power at its extremities'. These local power relations, he contends, are not reducible to laws, are open-ended, often are not codified or subject to definite protocols of enforcement. Foucault employs a bottom-up analysis from local power relations to 'global strategies' of power. He terms local power relations 'tactics' and places them within a general objective or bigger pattern — a 'strategy'. Thus, power relations in the therapy relationship would be tactics and would fall within a strategy of the power relations in psychiatry, social services and other institutional practices. He describes a two-way relationship between tactics and strategies: strategies condition or effect tactics and are conditioned or effected by them. Thus, the tactics of power in the therapy relationship are affected by, and in turn affect, the strategy of power relations within institutions. Similarly, the tactics used by particular models of therapy influence and are influenced by the tactics within therapy as a whole. Primary in Foucault's analyses are strategic objectives which render power relations intelligible in terms of a bigger pattern or a general aim. An example of these are the strategies of surveillance that emerged at the end of the nineteenth century and which Foucault described in *Discipline and Punish* (1977) and *Madness and Civilisation* (1977) and I describe later in section (b). These strategic objectives may be intentional or 'unintentional', as Foucault is not concerned with intention or consciousness; he describes them as 'great anonymous, almost unspoken strategies' (*The History of Sexuality*, Vol. 1, 1981, p. 95).

Power is not a property or a possession, but a strategy, a 'complex strategical situation', a 'multiplicity of power relations'. Where there is power, there is a multiplicity of resistances. These resistances have many forms and move around and transform. As Smart explains, 'Fortunately human existence . . . has escaped total subjection and subordination through forms of resistance to the exercise of power' (1985, p. 106). However, Foucault emphasises that the very existence of these resistances is often part of the justification for the continued use of the strategies of power. Thus, in therapy a client can resist the power of the exercising of disciplinary power by the therapist, but there is a danger that the therapist can overemphasise the client's agency to justify using their power oppressively.

Each of Foucault's analyses starts with a problem and seeks to investigate it by means of a case study or case history. He does not imply causation or the idea of progress, as in conventional historical accounts: he starts from the existence of a discourse and analyses it to make it intelligible, but without precluding other analyses. He avoids 'ideas' and rejects the notion of 'genres', or the necessary relation of discourses that exist at the same time. Similarly, he rejects the conventional historical notion of the 'march of reason' or necessary continuity or progress. Instead, he identifies 'discursive formations' from the grouping of 'discursive events', which are of the same style, are about the same concepts and support a common theme or strategy. This methodology is similar to the qualitative research methodology of thematic phenomenological analysis but also including functional analysis.

For Foucault, knowledges are social practices, and statements are recognised by their function and so cannot be identified in isolation. There is no priority for 'science' above other knowledge, and no knowledge independent of discursive formations, or independent of the function of the knowledge (see footnote 7). As Clegg (1989) explains, the meanings of discursive practices are the sites of power struggles: the function and meaning of language and how it is used is determined by the dynamics of power. Within therapy, discursive practices are the theories behind each model of therapy and the way in which they constitute the subjectivities[4] of therapist and client. For example, within psychodynamic therapy, discursive practices include the notion that the 'patient' has unconscious feelings and impulses which the therapist is superior at inferring and

---

4. 'Subjectivity' refers to individuals' sense of themselves and their way of understanding their relation to the world. This understanding will be through discourses that refer to and define an individual. Thus, a subject is the representation of an individual within language or discourse. Subjectivity refers to the way individuals talk and think about themselves. Post-structuralist subjectivity is precarious, contradictory and in process, constantly being reconstituted by discourse. The individual is always the site of conflicting forms of subjectivity.

understanding. This discourse then constitutes the subjectivities of an expert therapist and an unknowing client.

For Foucault, the analysis of power-knowledge relations is central to the analysis of power relations, because power and knowledge are inseparable and implicate and determine each other; knowledge is used to justify the exercise of power. He explains that 'there can be no possible exercise of power without a certain economy of discourses of truth which operate through and on the basis of this association' (*Power and Knowledge*, 1980, p. 93). This analysis follows the thesis, derived from Nietzsche, that power produces knowledge and that power and knowledge directly imply one another. Also following from this is the theory that the distinction between true or false is located in a political field; that what is deemed true is determined by operations of power and the function served by particular discourses. Foucault's analyses ask the questions 'What are the particular conditions under which these discourses arise? What are the relations of knowledge that make certain concepts possible?' Power and knowledge should be analysed with respect to how the relations of power define fields of knowledge and produce objects of knowledge. Truth is not a description of fact or of how the world 'really is'. Instead, truth is created by relations of power. Objects of knowledge are not given, but constructed. Foucault jettisons the ontological category of reality, questioning the existence of an objective 'reality'. Instead, he assumes no 'reality' outside of socially and politically constructed discourses. This follows the principles of social constructionism.

Foucault also focuses on the 'regimes of truth', the ensemble of rules according to which true and false are separated and specific effects of power attached to truth. He identifies in our society the 'regimes of truth': that scientific discourses are truth, that there is a 'will to truth', and that truth is a battleground. Foucault is concerned not with the theoretical status of discourses, with the privilege given to certain epistemological categories or types of knowledge, the division between science and non-science, but just with the conditions of their emergence. He analyses discursive practices:

> Ways of talking, thinking, feeling and acting that, when enacted, serve to reinforce, reproduce or support a given discourse and at the same time deny, disqualify or silence that which does not fit with that discourse. (Law, 1999, p. 119)

For Foucault, the circulation of power is intrinsically connected to the continual constitution and recreation of subjects (the representation of the individual in discourse: see footnote 4, p. 44). There are no rational unified human beings; no 'essence' of an individual is assumed to pre-exist social relations. Subjectivity is constituted through discursive practices. Here, the relationship between power and language is of prime importance. Identities are always being constructed and are relational and contextual rather than absolute. This process of identity construction concerns the circulation of power, how individuals are simultaneously undergoing and exercising the power that circulates. Foucault extends Lukes' third dimension of power (see Chapter 3) from the way power shapes individuals' interests to how it constitutes the individuals themselves. In contrast to Lukes, for Foucault there are no 'real' interests of individuals, prior to the operations of power.

In his earlier works (such as *Discipline and Punish,* 1977) Foucault concentrated on 'disciplinary techniques', on 'docile bodies' — how tactics and strategies of power governed and constituted subjects. In his later works he concentrated more on the constitution of the self and the techniques of the self, normative rules by which individuals constitute themselves by the 'stylisation of the self'. He suggests in his later work that individuals have much more agency than was suggested by his earlier concentration on 'docile bodies': here he focuses much more on resistance to power.

In summary, Foucault analyses the forms of knowledge and the relations of power through which humans have been constituted as subjects. He explains how humans govern themselves and others by the establishment of 'regimes of truth', and how a 'regime of rationality' constitutes rules and procedures for doing things. Similarly, certain discourses are given the status of 'truth' which then legitimate activities through the provision of reasons and principles. Rajchman (1985) explains that Foucault is a sceptic; his projects all question the self-evidence of a form of experience, knowledge or power, to free it and to open new possibilities for thought or action.

(b) The human sciences

For Foucault, the human sciences are of a special nature, being both 'positivist' (describing observable phenomena) and 'dialectical' (exploring metaphysical contradictions). For the first time, humans are both the subject and object of inquiry. Individuals' own knowledge of themselves is central to their definition. The human sciences try to specify what determines a person by revealing that what determines a person at the same time eludes the person's consciousness. So, with the emergence of the human sciences, thought is expanded to include that which is not conscious. At the same time, there is a constant movement in the human sciences to try and bring consciousness and thought together. Foucault contends that the instability of the human sciences is a consequence of the conditions of knowledge within which the human sciences operate. These conditions of knowledge are the reliance on examination of thought and consciousness, which are both the content of the knowledge and the way of making sense of the knowledge. The human sciences link the empirical questions of the contents of knowledge to the transcendental question of the conditions of knowledge. So, in therapy, the evidence on which theories are based is the content of consciousness, which provides both the content of the knowledge and the ways of making sense of this knowledge.

Foucault describes the conditions for the emergence of the human sciences through his analyses of the institutions of internment — the asylum, the clinic and the prison — all of which emerged simultaneously at the turn of the nineteenth century. Later the psychiatrist's couch emerged, which Foucault considered to be similarly part of the institutions of internment:

> The institutions of the asylum, the hospital, the prison and the psychiatrist's couch have constituted not only contexts within which relations of power have been formed and exercised but in addition 'laboratories' for the observation and documentation, from which bodies of knowledge have accumulated about the mad, the criminal, the sick and the 'sexual subject'. (Smart, 1985, p. 105)

Foucault's thesis is that the emergence and diffusion of the technologies of power exercised over life provided the appropriate conditions under which the human sciences could emerge. These technologies of power were, notably, the technologies of discipline and confession and their associated methods of assessment, examination, subjection, objectification and individualisation. In turn, the human sciences, drawing upon a conception of normality accorded scientificity by virtue of its derivation in the biological and medical sciences, contributed to an enhancement and refinement of the technologies of power. The attribution of 'truth' to discourses of science that included the human sciences gave justification for the technologies of power exercised over humans. The use of the human sciences to 'describe' what is 'normal' in humans has the effect of constituting subjects in this way. The effect of these technologies of power is the normalisation of subjects (see Fig. 4a).

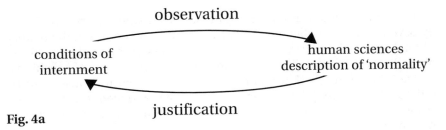

observation

conditions of
internment

human sciences
description of 'normality'

justification

Fig. 4a

An example of this normalisation was the classification of 'homosexuality' as a mental illness until very recently (1973 in America and 1992 in Europe), which gave the status of 'truth' to the idea that anything other than heterosexuality was abnormal. At the same time, this gave the legal system grounds to seek out and punish those defined 'homosexual' by, for example, the policing of 'cottaging' and such investigations as 'Operation Spanner', whereby adult men having consenting sex in a private house were charged. The more hidden result of the idea of the abnormality of non-heterosexuality is the result of many people considering heterosexuality to be the only option. Even though homosexuality has now been depathologised, the effects of its previous status as a disease linger on in the public consciousness and in many aspects of the law.

In Foucault's analysis of the institutions of internment, he describes how their regimes are founded upon similar disciplinary techniques, which is why he classes them together as one strategy of power. His thesis is thus that these institutions are central nodes in the network of power relations that mark out modernity[5] and support particular knowledges of the human sciences. He contends that these institutions are sites of 'dividing practices', of the mad and the sane, the sick and the healthy, and the criminals and the law-abiding.

Foucault explains in *Power and Knowledge* (1980) (reprinted in Lukes, 1986) that the human sciences represent the intersection of the discourses of rights and sovereign power (modernist/structural concepts of power) and of disciplinary power, of normalisation. They represent the intersection of the power of a central body over individuals using law, and the power of normalising discourses over individuals. The human sciences function as an arbitrating discourse between these discourses, a power and knowledge that the sanctity of science renders neutral. The status of science as 'truth' hides the political and social normalising functions of the knowledge in the human sciences. This can be seen particularly within psychiatry, where, within the powerful discourse of 'mental illness', the political and social normalising functions and implications are hidden behind the idea of scientific 'truth' (see Chapter 1).

(c) The history of madness

Foucault provides a counter-history of madness to the history sanctioned by psychiatry. He challenges the conventional conception of the history of madness — the march of reason and progress to the final recognition of madness as mental illness and the growth of knowledge of psychiatry. Instead, he contends that madness is a disparate entity constituted by different frameworks of its perception, and that the conception of madness as mental illness is a result of the convergence of internment and medicine, not objective truth.

Foucault is also interested to analyse the techniques by which mad people were subject to moral restraint and punishment in the asylums.

---

5. Modernity is the period of time described by Foucault where science is given the status of truth and objectivity and scientific discourses are central to the description of the world.

He identifies three disciplinary tactics: (1) the silencing of mad people by the observation and assessment of those with knowledge (the doctors), (2) self-discipline, and (3) discipline by mutual assessment of inmates and assessment by guardians. Foucault also notes that these techniques were similar to those used in pioneer prisons. He contends that these power relations took the form of a general network extending beyond the penal and psychiatric regimes; that the humanisation of the penal system and the emergence of the human sciences could be viewed together in the framework of the development of a new style of exercising power. The new style and new techniques are characterised by the shift in the target of punishment from the body to the personality or the soul. The same techniques were used to punish and reform criminals and mad people.

Foucault's analysis describes three methods by which the disciplinary techniques were put into operation: first, by hierarchical observation; second, by normalising judgement, and third, by examination and assessment. He explains that at the heart of all disciplinary systems there is a small penal mechanism to rectify deviations from the norm. The disciplinary penalty is corrective, aiming to decrease the range of deviation. The normalising judgement is passed less on behaviour than on the person behind the behaviour, the effect of which is to blur the boundaries between punishment, cure and corrective treatment and open the way for the knowledge of psychiatry and criminology to emerge.

(d) The history of sexuality

Foucault presents the domain of sexuality as one of the most important areas through which power has been exercised over life in modern Western societies. Foucault's thesis with regard to power over life is explained by Smart:

> The exercise of a pastoral 'caring' power over life in general (the population) and in particular (the individual subject) is presented as a fundamental or defining characteristic of modern societies and as a necessary precondition for the diffusion of capitalist economic relations throughout social life. (1985, p. 102)

Foucault observes that modern societies have shifted from sovereign power to governmental technologies of power directed towards an administration of the processes of life (e.g. of work and of reproduction), in order to optimise their political and economic utility with respect to the individual body and the population. Strategies of power are directed towards the control of individuals, to optimise the production and stability of the state. Foucault's analysis of sexuality is particularly useful to illustrate these technologies of power, as sexuality lies on the intersection of the two areas with which the strategies of power are concerned: that of the individual and the population.

The most important technique hypothesised by Foucault to achieve the surveillance and control of sexuality is that of 'confession'. Foucault underlines the importance of 'confession' as a technique for revealing details of sex, including acts and thoughts. Freud then extended the religious technique of confession to psychiatry. Psychoanalysis continued the popularity of confessional techniques. Smart (1985) explains Foucault's line of reasoning:

> The crystallisation of the doctor-patient relationship as the nexus
> for the identification and treatment of mental illness ultimately
> provided the space for Freud to introduce the technique of the
> confession in preference to the order of silence and observation.

This thus extended the area of control and surveillance from action and behaviour to thought. Foucault also notes that the dissemination of confessional techniques since the nineteenth century has been accompanied by attempts to circumvent them, for example, behaviourism. However, these other attempts can be seen similarly as a part of the disciplinary techniques available.

In summary, Foucault's thesis is that sexuality is an area where 'concrete arrangements' were arranged to ensure surveillance over life and the individual subject. For example, in schools the sexes were segregated. Medicine annexed 'sexual perversions', and definitions of these 'perversions' multiplied. Treatises in criminal justice and medicine intensified the public awareness of sex as a constant danger. Discourses about sex proliferated. The idea of confession as a disciplinary technique is important in considering power relations in therapy. The arena of therapy extends the power of normalisation from behaviour to the thoughts and feelings of the client, which are rendered vulnerable to judgement, control and normalisation.

Foucault and the context of therapy

Foucault's analyses of the human sciences, of the history of madness and of the history of sexuality all provide an analysis of the context in which therapy takes place. He describes the idea of the 'confession' as a disciplinary technique, and questions the objectivity of 'madness' as a category entailing treatment. His analyses force us to investigate the way in which psychotherapy can be a context for surveillance and disciplinary techniques of the self, of normalisation. He describes the ways in which power can be observed in the practices within psychiatry and psychotherapy, which attempt to normalise individuals.

Foucault's notion of the stylisation of the self is particularly relevant to issues of power in therapy, as therapy explicitly sets out to reconstitute the self, according to normalising rules. This can be observed particularly in the principles of Cognitive Behaviour Therapy (CBT), where the aim is to reconstitute the client according to 'rational' and 'helpful' ways of thinking (see Chapter 5). However, Foucault does not place a value judgement on these practices of power, and he emphasises the productive aspects of power, explained by Butler as 'the way in which regulative practices produce the subjects they come to subjugate' (1990, p. 98). In emphasising the productive aspects of power, Foucault is stressing the impossibility of escaping relations of power; that subjects are always constituted in relation to others, and that this mutual influence and intersubjectivity is not necessarily negative. This points to the importance of examining the ethical value-bases behind each therapy.

He also stresses the resistances that will always be present wherever there is power. To investigate power in therapy from this perspective, it would be necessary to explore how both the therapist and the client actively constitute themselves in the therapy relationship within the normalising rules influencing their roles, considering the positive and negative effects of how the relationship influences and constitutes each subject. Thus, in the following three chapters, I examine the effect of the theories of therapy on both the therapist's power and the client's resistance, and consider how the theories constitute the positions of both therapist and client, and their ability to influence each other.

Foucault's analyses are historically and contextually specific, and to understand the context of psychotherapy it is necessary to explore the techniques of power involved, particularly with regard to the techniques of the self, the ways that individuals constitute themselves according to discourses of normalisation. Thus, in the following three chapters, I investigate the rhetoric in the various models of therapy to explore their use of normalising discourses.

Rose (1985) analyses the conditions of the emergence of psychology as an academic discipline, following Foucault's method. He notes that, far from psychology developing a science of the 'normal' which was then applied to the pathological or 'abnormal', psychological knowledge of the individual was constituted around the pole of abnormality. In fact, psychology specifically set itself up to deal with the problems posed for social systems and procedures by dysfunctional conduct. From the origins of psychology, the pole of 'normal-abnormal' was set around social efficiency and need for social regulation.

Rose further noted that, for academic psychology to have credence as a scientific discipline, it had to lay claims to truth. Psychology laid claims to this by the study of individual differences, and the consequences of this were that

> The abnormality around which individual psychology was organised was not an abnormality of a life process, or one specifiable in terms of ease or dis-ease. It was an abnormality in terms of a

> norm of functioning specified by particular social apparatuses. The
> unease which enabled the normativity of individual psychology to
> be established was constituted by the objectives of government
> rather than the vicissitudes of the psyche. (1985, p. 229)

In other words, psychology got off the ground as an accepted discipline
only when it abandoned its project of theories of cognitive function and
succeeded in producing norms of regulating social behaviour. Pilgrim and
Treacher further explain the result of a Foucaultian analysis of the 'psy'
professions, saying:

> During the twentieth century, with the decline of segregative control
> in institutions, coercive power has become less and less relevant.
> Within this analysis, psychological therapies, counselling and health
> education are examples, par excellence, of a new type of moral
> regulation favoured by government and public. (1992, p. 190)

Thus, from its conception, psychology has gained its status as a form of
regulation of social control, an agent of the state with a normalising
function. With the decline of the institution, the role of therapy in
normalisation has become more and more important.

Rose's analysis points to the relationship between power and the
production of knowledge with which Foucault was concerned. Rose's
analysis, in contrast to most written on therapy and power (as described
in Chapter 2), seems not to adopt a moral stance towards the holding of
power, but instead seeks to describe a situation. He concentrates on
strategies of power, on ways in which the profession of psychology
legitimised its knowledge base and thus gained power.

Pilgrim and Treacher (1992) examine the historical context further
by looking at the origins of clinical psychology as a profession. Following
the same theme as Rose (1985) in terms of psychology as an agent of
control, they point to the scientificism of psychology as a defence against
accusations of performing the function of social control. They explain:

> Psychologists . . . could play out a highly political role in terms of
> the management of the population, whilst at the same time
> disowning such a role by pointing to their 'disinterested' scientific
> training and credentials. (Pilgrim and Treacher, 1992, p. 30)

They further contend that 'Scientificism as a justificatory ideology is still
a dominant strand in the profession today' (p. 31). This is demonstrated
by the emphasis within the profession on being a 'scientist practitioner'.
Pilgrim and Treacher point out that this conception of clinical psychology
is neither accurate (with respect to the importance of research in clinical
psychology) nor useful (in that it leaves moral and epistemological
questions unanswered). They explain the history of clinical psychology

training, which was originally set up to train psychometricians, and, although clinical psychologists now spend most of their time conducting therapy as opposed to conducting psychometric assessments, the duration and philosophy of training has not changed substantially to reflect this. In particular, 'Above all else the person of the clinical psychologist never became a legitimate area of discussion within psychology' (p. 97). This critique is particularly relevant to cognitive behaviour therapy (see Chapter 5).

Critiques of Foucault

The most vocal critiques of Foucault have come from feminism. However, there have been a variety of responses to Foucault from feminist theorists, ranging from developments of post-modernist feminist theories (Weedon, 1987) to challenges to Foucault's usefulness, particularly with regard to feminist politics. Generally, some aspects of his work and ideas have been welcomed by feminists, such as his questioning of the notion of objective truth and his rejection of the essential self; but other aspects have been disputed, particularly his relativism with regard to value judgements and what has been perceived as the lack of agency of individuals.

McNay (1992) asks two questions for feminists using Foucault. First, she asks, with the move from unitary to fragmented subjects, where does this leave social agency? The idea of fragmented subjects follows from the way subjects are continually constituted in relationships and social context. This calls into question the idea of an essential self, a unified individual. She asks whether this move leaves notions of individual responsibility and agency behind. Second, with the 'relativist' suspension of value judgements, where does this leave emancipatory politics? Here the question is whether, without taking a moral stance toward the exercising of power, the value-base behind emancipatory politics, which criticises the oppressive and dominating results of the exercise of power, is lost.

In response to the first question, she suggests that in his earlier works Foucault refers to 'docile bodies' and reduces individuals to passive recipients of disciplinary power as opposed to active agents. However, she contends that in his final work Foucault goes some way to address the limitations of subjects not being agents, by elaborating his notion of the self. He adds technologies of subjectification to his earlier focus on technologies of domination, through which individuals actively fashion their own identities within the social context and respond to rules or values regarding their behaviour. This suggests a more dynamic relationship between social structures and individuals. Here practices of the self are both ways in which individuals police themselves and ways in which they resist and ensure their freedom. She explains:

> Individuals are no longer conceived as docile bodies in the grip of
> an inexorable disciplinary power, but as self-determining agents

who are capable of challenging and resisting the structures of domination in modern society. (McNay, 1992, p. 4)

However, McNay suggests that, by not prioritising how much different techniques of the self are imposed to different levels, Foucault's notion of the stylisation of the self hides the force of cultural norms. She questions Foucault's failure to link practices of the self to gender issues, and she contends that here feminism can inform his work.

The notion of an essential self is often a premise in counselling and therapy, particularly in person-centred therapy. Psychoanalysis theorises a fragmented subject. However, all three models of therapy that I go on to consider in detail theorise an already constituted subject, one constituted fundamentally through childhood experiences. Foucault's theories remind us to consider the ways in which subjects continually reconstitute themselves through relationships, so that the aim becomes one of helping individuals to constitute themselves in the most advantageous ways possible (see section on 'Deconstruction and therapy' later in this chapter) as opposed to refinding a former essential self. Person-centred therapy theorises this in terms of the concept of 'actualisation' (see Chapter 6).

Butler (1992) answers the reservations of feminists who are concerned about Foucault's lack of emphasis on the notion of agency. She suggests that to presume agency presupposes a constituted unitary subject, a concept that she believes is responsible for the route of essentialism[6] and subordination of women. She explains:

> But if we agree that politics and power already exist at the level at which the subject and its agency are articulated and made possible, then agency can only be presumed at the cost of refusing to inquire into its construction . . . For the subject to be a pregiven point of departure for politics is to defer the question of political construction and regulation of the subject itself; for it is important to remember that subjects are constituted through exclusion, that is, through the creation of a domain of deauthorised subjects, presubjects, figures of abjection, populations erased from view. (Butler, 1992, p. 13)

Thus, Butler questions the process by which subjects (see footnote 4, p. 44) are formed and suggests the necessity to analyse this process, particularly with respect to what the process of subjectivity excludes. Butler concurs with Foucault's concept of the fragmented subject and questions agency, suggesting that Foucault's analysis is useful for feminist politics.

---

6. In the context of feminism, 'essentialism' refers to the belief or assumption of an essential, innate, usually biological, or sometimes psychological, difference between men and women, which is then used to justify the different positions of men and women in society with respect to power.

Butler (1997) further extends Foucault's notions of power to consider the effect of power relations intra-psychically. She examines how relations of power form the subject, and how no subject emerges without a passionate attachment to those on whom the individual is dependent, thus rendering the child vulnerable to subordination and exploitation. Subordination is the linguistic condition of the individual's existence and agency as a subject. She describes the double bind of how the process of becoming a subject (subjection) signifies both the process of subordination by power and the condition of possibility for agency. Subjects are constituted by relations of power but have agency only as a result of being constituted as subjects. However, she emphasises the lack of necessary continuity between the power that is a condition of a subject and the power wielded by the subject.

A subject is defined by the capacity for reflexivity. For Nietzsche, self-knowing is a consequence of self-punishment. Similarly, for Butler, reflexivity is self-inspection, an internalisation of norms, a prohibition of desire and self-subordination. Subjection is simultaneously the formation and the regulation of the subject. This follows Foucault, who formulates resistance as an effect of the very power that it is said to oppose. The consequence of this is explained by Butler: 'the strategic question for Foucault is, then, how can we work with the power relations by which we are worked, and in whose direction?' (1997, p. 100). Thus, she demonstrates the inevitability of relations of power, and particularly of domination and subjection, but also the inevitability of the accompanying possibility of agency and resistance. This idea fits with the philosophy of most models of therapy, where the aim is to inquire into how individuals have come to be who they are, and how they have been subjected. However, at the same time, individuals are held responsible for their behaviour and the aim is change which can be likened to resistance.

In response to the second question about the absence of values, McNay (1992) also points out that, despite a clear commitment to some form of political change and commitment to individual freedom, and resisting disciplinary power, Foucault refuses to outline the normative assumptions upon which he would advocate social change. She suggests that these assumptions are necessary not to constrain individuals, but to prevent abuses of power, and she emphasises that feminism must hold on to values and a commitment to emancipatory social change. Similarly, Grimshaw (1993) challenges Foucault's lack of moral and political base to his work. While seeking to be descriptive, Foucault said that he was disturbed by the implications of his 'neutral' theory of power. Grimshaw suggests that, without distinguishing malign from benign forms of power, we do not know what power to resist.

In considering power in therapy from a Foucaultian perspective, there can be a dilemma of providing a description without any value judgement about whether power is helpful or oppressive in this context, and in what ways. There are clear values in the foundation of the practice of therapy, the most obvious being the desire to help the client and improve the client's quality of life. Without any judgement about how power can impact on this, analyses do not suggest any way forward or any political action. Smail (1987) notes the dangers of this moral relativism and the dangers of abandoning any notion of 'truth'. However, at other times Foucault is clear about his political agenda (for example in the forward to Deleuze and Guattari, 1984), and indeed, when discussing therapy, suggests that the aim must be to avoid domination. Rajchman (1985) suggests that sceptical freedom is the political intent of Foucault's analyses — a constant questioning of dogmatic unity, truths or prescriptive policies. Within therapy, this would suggest an attitude of questioning and scepticism towards any theories that prescribe how individuals should be.

Fish (1999, p. 67) cites Foucault, suggesting a way forward in dealing with relations of power:

> I do not think that a society could exist without power relations, if by that one means the strategies by which individuals try to direct and control the conduct of others. The problem, then, is not to try to dissolve them in the utopia of completely transparent communication but to acquire the rules of law, the management techniques, and also the morality, the ethos, the practice of the self, that will allow us to play these games of power with as little domination as possible. (Foucault, 1980, p. 298)

Following this statement, Fish (1999) asserts that therapists cannot eliminate the power that is inherent in the socially constituted structure of their role (their *role power*). However, he does suggest three ways to try and avoid domination in therapy. First, therapists should support the client's communication and try to ensure adequate reciprocal influence with the therapist. Second, the therapist's use of power and domination should be monitored by both the therapists themselves and others, such as supervisors and institutional regulators. Third, he stresses the importance of the availability to the client of powerful means of redress outside the therapy relationship (such as procedures for complaints, suing, etc.). This third suggestion points to the importance of methods to increase the client's *role power*.

Deleuze and Guattari's concept of power

Deleuze and Guattari (1984) follow the post-structuralist ideas of Foucault concerning power, while being very explicit about their value-base. In addition, they are important in considering issues of power in therapy, because of their critique of the concept of the Oedipus complex. This critique has particular implications for psychodynamic therapy, but it also can be applied to other models, where the aim of therapy can be seen to repress emotions or desire. I would suggest that their critique can equally be applied to cognitive behaviour theory, where clients are encouraged to repress feelings in favour of cognition, to trust rationality rather than what feels right. In this sense, the aims behind psychoanalysis and CBT are similar: that impulses and feelings are not to be trusted, but need to be analysed and subjected to the test of rationality.

Deleuze and Guattari, in *Anti-Oedipus: Capitalism and Schizophrenia* (1984), provide a critique of the basis of psychoanalytic theory, the Oedipus complex.[7] They contend that the Oedipus myth prohibits incest, thus implicitly suggesting that people desire incest. However, they claim that this provides a displacement of what is threatening to society, which is desire itself, each individual's own wants and feelings, which may conflict with the stability of society. The Oedipus myth gives a justification for psychic repression of individuals. The authors suggest that this psychic repression is necessary for social repression, and they put together ideas from Marx and Nietzsche to create a theory of social and psychic repression. They hypothesise that social repression is dependent on desire through sexual repression and on the family as the agent of psychic repression. They further elaborate this interrelationship between psychic and social repression, saying:

> Social repression needs psychic repression precisely in order to form docile subjects and to ensure the reproduction of the social formation including its repressive structure. (p. 118)

They suggest that, by substituting incest for desire, the interest for social production is evident, 'for the latter could not otherwise ward off desire's potential for revolt and revolution' (p. 120).

They problematise the association of desire with acquisition, and claim that instead desire is productive, producing reality. As Foucault explains in the Preface, 'The individual is the product of power. What is needed is to "de-individualise" by means of multiplication and displacement, diverse combinations' (p. xiv). Deleuze and Guattari (1984) propose *schizoanalysis* as a solution — lines of escape from the schizophrenic process as a potential for revolution. Here, the subject is decentred and desire becomes revolutionary. They explain:

> Once we forget about our egos a non-neurotic form of politics becomes possible, where singularity and collectivity are no longer at odds with each other; and where collective expressions of desire are possible. (p. xxi)

Instead of 'neurotic' dependencies on professionals, they suggest mutual

---

7. The Oedipus conflict was a key stage in the development of a child for Freud. He hypothesised that the male child, who loves his mother, realises he is in competition for his mother's love with his father. He resolves the conflict by deferring to paternal authority.

self-care, with healing being a process of ego-loss, a need to form a collective subjectivity. They claim revolutionary potential for desiring-machines (which replace individuals), following lines of escape from psychic repression. They explain: 'capitalist society can endure many manifestations of interest, but not one manifestation of desire, which would be enough to make its fundamental structures explode' (p. 379).

Thus, for Deleuze and Guattari, power is involved not just in how subjects are constituted, but in creating the myth of unitary subjects[8] and the emphasis on individualism. Their theory would question the politics of individual therapy, and the implicit assumption (in some models of therapy such as CBT) of the goal of the unified rational subject. In contrast to Foucault, Deleuze and Guattari are clear about the Marxist values that inform their theory and suggest a clear way forward politically. Foucault in the Preface explains this value-base, saying:

> The major enemy, the strategic adversary is fascism . . . the fascism in us all, in our heads and in our everyday behaviour, the fascism that causes us to love power, to desire the very thing that dominates and exploits us. (p. xiii)

He suggests that Deleuze and Guattari's theory is an introduction to the non-fascist life. Whereas Foucault does not see it as his job to suggest a way forward, for fear of becoming prescriptive, Deleuze and Guattari make clear their value-base, the foundation of which is the fight against the constraining of the individual, and desire. While this value-base is implicit within Foucault's work, Deleuze and Guattari are able to use post-structuralist ideas to create a value-base and foundation for political action.

Deconstruction and therapy

Deconstruction aims to unpack the assumptions and consequences behind discourses or theory. Deconstructive strategies have been used within both psychology and psychotherapy. Deconstruction has influenced ideas about psychotherapy, most notably with new approaches to therapy based on these ideas, such as narrative therapy, particularly the ideas of Michael White (e.g. White and Epston, 1990). Narrative therapy aims to examine the function and effect of narratives that clients use to describe their life and to rewrite more helpful narratives. In 'Deconstruction and Psychotherapy', Parker (1999) presents various ways of applying concepts of deconstruction to theory and practice in psychotherapy. He clearly advocates notions of deconstruction from a

---

8. The myth of unitary subjects is the idea that a subject is an essential self that is consistent within itself and over time. In contrast, Foucault emphasises the way in which subjects are continually constructed within relations of power and social and political contexts.

moral standpoint and as a critique against power in therapy. Here, post-structural ideas are used from a clear value-base of justice. He explains:

> Forms of psychotherapy which take their cue from psychiatric or psychological systems, whether these are behaviourist, cognitive or psychoanalytic, also take for granted descriptions of pathology which often oppress people as they pretend to help them. (Parker, 1999, p. 2)

He then invokes deconstruction as a way forward elaborated by Derrida by investigating how our understanding of problems is located in discourse. He suggests:

> We must then reflect on how we make and may remake our lives through moral-political projects which are embedded in a sense of justice (Derrida, 1994) rather than give psychiatric diagnoses. (p. 2)

Parker further explains the task of the deconstructing therapist:

> To locate the problem in certain cultural practices, and to comprehend the role of patterns of power in setting out positions for people which serve to reinforce the idea that they can do nothing about it themselves. (1999, p. 3)

He emphasises the lack of a 'right answer' in deconstructing psychotherapy, saying 'To be "critical", then, does not mean finding the correct standpoint, but it means understanding how we come to stand where we are' (p. 4). He argues that deconstructing approaches to therapy connect the personal and the political without reducing one to the other. One of the aims of deconstruction in therapy is 'to trace the ways oppression is reconfigured and reproduced at a personal level' (p. 5). He also emphasises the importance of the means of therapy being consistent with the ends. This suggests the need to explore the effects of power in the therapy relationship, if we assume that the result of therapy should be for the client to feel powerful, or at least not further disempowered. Deconstructing therapies also take ideas and concepts from Foucault, particularly his analysis of power in psychology. Parker (1999) explains Foucault's contribution; he showed 'how the twin tendencies of discipline and confession lock people together in such a way that the discipline of psychology becomes seen as a necessity and is then able to pose a solution' (p. 9).

Parker also criticises the rhetoric of 'empowerment' often used in speaking about therapy. He explains:

> Even the word 'empowerment' betrays something of the position of the expert who thinks that they have been able to move an enlightened step beyond 'helping' people but cannot give up the idea

that it is possible to bend down to lift someone lesser than themselves up a step, to give them a little empowerment. (1999, pp. 9–10)

He suggests that deconstruction be used in three ways: deconstruction in therapy as part of a process of exploring people's narratives; deconstruction as psychotherapy in the reworking of the therapy relationship to address issues of power; and deconstructing therapy to reflect on the enterprise itself. In this book I attempt both to deconstruct the enterprise of therapy and to suggest ways in which therapy can be deconstructive by addressing issues of power.

Discourses of 'empowerment' in therapy include the notions of 'collaboration' or 'transparency', which are deconstructed by Lowe (1999). He asks:

> How collaborative can collaboration be, and how transparent can transparency be, if they are institutionalised within a particular mode of practice? It is one thing to offer clients a voice within a professional therapeutic discourse, but it might be quite another thing to allow them a discourse of their own. (p. 82)

He further suggests that these discourses, rather than being 'empowering' to clients, are in fact 'misempowering', by 'adding new tools to the armoury of the already powerful'(p. 83).

Deconstructing therapy involves a clear ethical position. Larner (1999) suggests that a deconstructing therapist must be both modern and post-modern; to deconstruct therapy requires positioning both inside and outside the system of therapy. He suggests that it is possible to be a therapist and use power ethically, by claiming that the therapist's power is balanced by the ethical stance towards the other. He describes the essence of this ethical stance as an acknowledgement of each person's uniqueness, a respect for the otherness of a separate being. He stresses the importance in ethical psychotherapy of privileging the voice of the client. Further, he contends that ethical practice 'requires a location not a dissolution of the subject' (p. 47). He suggests that the therapist needs to be both powerful and non-powerful in the therapy relationship — powerful against violence in the ethical relation, yet non-powerful to allow the other to speak. He explains further:

> The conscious movement of the therapist towards the other as an ethical stance allows a true dialogue of unequals, in which both therapist and client are powerful *and* non-powerful . . . The ethical challenge in psychotherapy is to minimise the therapist's potential to violate the other through therapy . . . this is the potential violence of theory, authority, expertise and technology to override the client's contribution to their life narrative. (Larner, 1999, p. 48, original emphasis)

The importance of ethics for the therapist follows from the link between power and responsibility. Larner emphasises the ethical principle of justice and responsibility. He suggests that deconstruction as justice is to be found wherever therapists are responsibly questioning their own foundations and institutions. He points out that Derrida does not renounce knowledge and power, but links them to responsibility.

Ethics and values are at the foundation of a therapy relationship and are the clearest indicators as to whether 'therapeutic' is accurately descriptive of a helpful relationship. O'Reilly Byrne and Colgan McCarthy (1999) use the existence of an ethical therapy relationship as a defining feature of therapy. They claim:

> In our view a discourse can be said to be therapeutic to the extent
> that the exchange between participants foregrounds the potential
> for reciprocity of perspectives and mutual respect. (p. 87)

They advocate an approach to a deconstructing psychotherapy which focuses on ambivalence and does not aim to overthrow ambivalence with colonisation or certainty. They focus on discourses that constrain individual or collective liberty and they describe their approach as 'a deconstructive strategy that loosens the hold of singular discourses over a personal life' (p. 97).

Deconstruction concerns the exposing of power. Foucault noted that 'power is tolerable only on the condition that it masks a substantial part of itself, its success is proportional to its ability to hide its own mechanisms' (1981, p. 86). Swan (1999) argues against the claim that all therapy is oppressive by suggesting that this view misses the power of oppression operating at a very local level on people's feelings about themselves, i.e. the ways in which subordination and regulation are internalised within the subject. Here she refers to Foucault's descriptions of the effects of power on the stylisation of the self and seems to suggest that therapy can help individuals to deconstruct these effects of power. She suggests that therapy can be a means to politicise personal relations as a stepping-stone to political action. Individuals can use therapy to deconstruct their own strategies of internal regulation and to understand the way in which they have incorporated these regulations, and then to move on to challenge the wider context of these regulations.

Others suggest that therapy can be used to reframe disciplinary discourses with the discourse of resistance. Madigan (1999) aims in therapy to bring people away from totalising discourses of diagnoses and harmful disciplinary practices and to help people to arm themselves with discourses of resistance. Similarly, Smail suggests the therapist's job can be 'subversive'. He describes this job as follows:

> To help reveal the meaning of experience, to 'demystify' it by
> liberating it from the normalising ideology of our time and

> explicating it as the inevitable and reasonable response of embodied
> beings to an encompassing spatio-temporal world. The subversive
> psychotherapist is concerned not with engineering a disciplinary
> norm, but with making space for diversity and eccentricity . . . In
> this way, one sides with the person rather than with the social world,
> helping to drag out his or her internalised norms so that they can
> be seen for what they are: the external disciplinary apparatus of a
> fundamentally oppressive social organisation. (Smail, 1987, p. 401)

However, others are dubious about the potential for a deconstructing, resisting therapy. Riikonen and Vataja (1999) suggest that we do not know what psychotherapy really is and so we cannot deconstruct it. Further, they contend that promoting mental well-being relates to the happenings of everyday life, not to 'therapy'.

The foundation of this book rests on the values and ethics of deconstruction, of justice and responsibility, to resist domination and totalising discourses and to deconstruct the discourses behind models of therapy. Given that people who are distressed often choose to go for help in therapy, it is our duty and responsibility, as therapists, to deconstruct our practices and to be clear about the ethics, values and effects of the discourses and practices we use.

Syntheses of structuralist and post-structuralist ideas

Both structural and post-structural concepts of power can help us to explore issues of power in therapy. Structural concepts remind therapists of long-standing relations of domination and submission between groups of people which have led to relatively stable (but changeable) structures of power relations. Here contributions from the study of sociology can inform therapists' work and help them to understand individuals in social positions (*societal power*). These correspond to the domains of power described by Cromwell and Olson (1975) as *power bases* and *power outcomes* (see Chapter 1). In addition, structuralist ideas remind us of political value-bases which inform our deconstruction of power relations. Lukes' three dimensions of power are a useful way to conceptualise power from this perspective, and remind us how structures of power affect people on an ideological level, by shaping their interests.

Post-structuralist ideas, in contrast, can add a fourth dimension to the analysis of power. They emphasise the individual in social relation to others and the constitution of individuals by the relations of power. The structural notion of individuals defined by their place in society is supplemented in post-structural ideas by the notion of agency of individuals. This widens the scope of analysis from a radical environmental behaviourism (where individuals are determined totally by structures of power) to a consideration of the internal life and histories of individuals and their relationships. These ideas also describe the *power processes* described by Cromwell and Olson (1975) (see Chapter 1). It could be useful to have a model to combine the useful parts of all these concepts of power, and there have been some attempts to do this.

There are long-standing debates about the primacy of structure or agency. More recently, various theorists have argued that each is important and irreducible to the other, and have proposed ways to investigate power while bearing both in mind. Archer (1995) proposes an approach that she terms 'morphogenetic'. She suggests that structure, culture and agency are always involved and cannot be reduced to each other. Deleuze and Guattari (1984) also propose a synthesis between individuals and structures, while at the same time not presuming a rational unified subject. They provide a theory for the interrelationship between structures of power (particularly capitalism) and power on a micro level, between individuals and between different parts of an individual in self-regulation (or psychic repression). Like Archer (1995), they stress that both structures and agency are important: neither can be reduced to the other. Individuals determine structures, and structures determine individuals. These models are helpful to remind us that the levels of both structures and individuals need to be considered in a useful analysis of power relations.

Pulling together various areas of Foucault's work also provides an opportunity to synthesise structural and post-structural ideas. Madigan (1999) suggests that, although Foucault concentrates on power as being ubiquitous, he also acknowledges that relations of power produce dominant ideas and even structures of power (although these are not permanently fixed or completely determined subjects). He explains that, for Foucault,

> Power does not come from a central authority, is non-conspiratorial, and indeed non-orchestrated; yet it nonetheless produces and normalises bodies to serve prevailing relations of dominance and subordination. (Madigan, 1999, pp. 156–7)

Thus, within Foucault's writings there is a constant tension between structures of power and domination and individual agency, with a concentration in his earlier works on structures, and in his later works on the constitution of the self and the agency of the self in resistance.

The project of deconstruction can use concepts from both modernism and post-modernism. Lowe (1999) emphasises the lack of discontinuity between modernism and post-modernism and suggests the model of a 'climate of problematisation' for 'a context or site for critically rethinking discourses of particular fields without being reduced to a competition between modern and post-modern ideas' (p. 73). Some critical psychoanalytic theorists combine psychoanalysis and post-structural feminism to consider both structures and agency. These theories are presented in Chapter 7.

Conclusion

In this chapter I have elaborated post-structural concepts of power and considered how they can be applied to the issue of power in the therapy relationship. They provide a fourth dimension to the three-dimensional analysis of power from Lukes (see Chapter 3). The syntheses of structural and post-structural approaches described above explain the theoretical underpinnings for my analysis of power in the following chapters. In addition, the ethics of Foucault and of deconstruction, of constant questioning, particularly of 'taken-for-granted' assertions and truths, is the approach from which I examine the models of therapy in the following chapters.

Chapter 5

Cognitive Behaviour Therapy: the obscuring of power in the name of science

Introduction

Hawton et al. (1989) describe the evolution of Cognitive Behaviour Therapy (CBT) from its beginnings in behaviour therapy following the experimental work concerning classical and operant conditioning principles. They describe how in the 1970s the efficacy of behavioural treatments was established and the emphasis began to move to those patients who did not respond to strictly behavioural treatment. It was hypothesised that cognitive factors were involved. Thus, cognitive approaches to treatment began to be developed, from Meichenbaum's (1977) self-instructional training to Beck's (1976) cognitive therapy. Two general principles in CBT are the emphasis on (1) expressing concepts in operational terms (i.e. in ways which lead to action) and (2) empirically validating treatment. In this chapter the focus will be on CBT mainly as described by Beck and others using his ideas, as this is the most popular form of CBT used by therapists in Great Britain. Ellis's Rational Emotive Therapy will not be considered.

Principles

Trower et al. (1988) present an overview of the principles behind CBT. They describe the focus on thinking as the cause and solution of clients' difficulties, saying 'People rarely come to counselling complaining about their thinking, although their self-defeating thinking is often a major reason for their difficulties' (p. 1). They describe the central tenet of CBT as being that it is not events that produce bad feelings, but the way the events are appraised. CBT asserts that when people hold unrealistic or negative beliefs about themselves or their experiences emotional upset will result, and if this negative thinking is extreme or persistent it may lead to an emotional disorder. CBT distinguishes between ordinary fleeting thoughts, or automatic thoughts (Beck, 1976), and the underlying beliefs and assumptions that give rise to the automatic thoughts. The principles underlying CBT are, first, that the way an event is appraised (or the thoughts about the event) determines the emotions about it, and, second, that extreme and distressing emotions characterising disorders such as anxiety and depression are the result of unrealistic and negative beliefs. Finally, by altering these beliefs, emotional disturbance can be reduced.

Task of therapist

Trower et al. (1988) explain the steps involved in CBT. Primarily, it is the therapist's task to help clients become aware of the thoughts that are mediating their distress and to explain the cognitive model in terms of how their way of thinking produces distress and can be changed. Having checked that the client's goal is to reduce their distress, the therapist then helps the client to modify their thoughts by encouraging the client to treat the thoughts as hypotheses and to search for evidence to disprove the unrealistic and negative thoughts. Finally, the client is helped to replace the negative thoughts with positive ones, via the process of cognitive restructuring, and to act on the basis of them. Behavioural tasks are incorporated into therapy as a way of testing evidence and in an attempt to directly change beliefs by behaviours that contradict the beliefs. In CBT, the therapist can also use the relationship with the client to examine the beliefs and thoughts the client has about how they are in relationships. Trower et al. (1988) also emphasise that the aim of CBT is to teach the client to think not positively, but realistically. They point out that when things go wrong it would be irrational to be positive about that situation, but CBT helps people to avoid cognitive distortions such as generalising, globalising and personalising difficult situations and to take a more realistic perspective. They suggest that the role of the cognitive behaviour therapist is to 'show empathy and understanding of her client's predicament, yet help the client to put what has happened to him in a realistic perspective' (p. 7). With respect to the therapist–client relationship, Trower et al. point out that the role of the therapist is as educator or skills-trainer, and therapy is a collaborative endeavour.

Scientific method

CBT treatment is described as an experiment to test out hypotheses made from the original formulation formed at assessment. As hypotheses are tested the formulation is modified in the light of new information. Diaries are often used to collect self-report data from patients and the rating of symptoms and feelings is highly regarded. This evidence can be used to monitor progress and to provide realistic evaluation of how treatment is progressing. This demonstrates the emphasis in CBT on the importance of what the patient has achieved as opposed to how the patient is feeling about treatment.

Power imbalance in the therapy relationship

I have identified three aspects to the power imbalance in the therapy relationship: the power imbalance inherent in roles of 'therapist' and 'client' (*role power*), the personal history of the therapist and particularly the client with respect to the experience of power and powerlessness (*historical power*) and the power distribution with respect to the structural positions in society of the client and therapist (*societal power*) (see Chapter 1).

Power in the roles of therapist and client (*role power*)

Appeal to science

Cognitive behaviour therapy is based on the claim that the cause of distress lies in the individual's maladaptive thinking. The therapist has the knowledge about how to think in a more helpful way, and this knowledge rests on research evidence. The authority (or part of the *power base* – Cromwell and Olson, 1975; see Chapter 1) of the therapist rests on an appeal to science. The whole basis of the model is strongly founded on principles of modernism and the rationality of science. 'Knowledge' and research 'evidence' are not questioned but are presented as fact, and the therapist is assumed to be in an objective position to present this knowledge. From a Foucaultian perspective, CBT is rife with 'regimes of truth', normalising principles on which the 'right' or 'helpful' way to think are based. The focus on 'realism' can be used to discount or challenge the feelings or views of the client, who can then be accused of being prey to 'cognitive distortions'. Rationality is a clear value behind CBT, and the irrational is discounted or challenged.

Objectivity of the CBT therapist

Within CBT literature there is some caution about the objectivity of the therapist. Marshall (1996) points out that the therapist's authority leads to ethical implications that therapists have a duty to consider. She also emphasises the importance of supervision to ensure ethical practice and to ensure that the therapist's agenda does not impinge on the therapeutic relationship. She stresses the danger of therapists using their power to fulfil their own needs in the therapy relationship whereas the aim should be to use this power to help the client. The assumption in the CBT model is that the therapist can be in an objective position to decide scientifically what is best for the client. Thus, the aim of supervision here is to ensure that the therapist is acting from this neutral position, rather than from a position in the therapy relationship where the client could be used to fulfil the therapist's needs. Given the philosophy of the CBT model, however, it is not apparent how a focus on self-awareness in supervision could be accommodated (and it is certainly not theorised as being part of the model), particularly if supervision were a process by which the therapist and supervisor joined forces to decide what was in the best interests of the client.

Within other models of therapy, the self-awareness of the therapist is prioritised by encouragement to engage in personal therapy. This is not the case with CBT. Darongkamas et al. (1994) surveyed clinical psychologists working in the NHS in the UK, 41% of whom were cognitive behavioural therapists. Of the whole sample, 41% had had personal therapy, but only 20% of CBT therapists had had personal therapy. Of the CBT therapists who had had therapy, only 11% (two respondents) had chosen to see a CBT therapist and none of the clinical psychologists using other models of therapy had chosen a CBT therapist. As Rowan (1994) comments about the CBT therapists, 'What is good enough for their clients is not, apparently, good enough for themselves'.

The possibility of being in a neutral objective position is not problematised. It is clear that the concept of power referred to here is one in which the therapist is assumed to possess the power and power is unidirectional, characteristics of a structural model of power (see Chapter 3). However, unlike structural models of power, it is not assumed that this imbalance of power is necessarily negative. Instead, the power imbalance is justified, legitimised — again with the appeal to the rationality of science and the knowledge of the therapist. This appeal to science is reminiscent of Hobbes and Weber (see Chapter 3).

Telford and Farrington (1996) suggest that the therapist is not in a neutral position but is part of the therapy relationship. 'Cognitive behaviourists must wake up to the fact that the notion of the therapist as a neutral onlooker is no longer acceptable within therapy' (p. 149). Here, there is some acknowledgement that 'objectivity' has been questioned and that the possibility of a therapist being a neutral scientist whose values are not involved is dangerous. However, the full implications of this problematising of objectivity are not explored with respect to either the knowledge base of CBT or the therapist's position in the relationship. The inconsistencies in the questioning yet acceptance of the authority of the therapist are not explored either.

Spinelli (1994) discusses the notion of the 'objectivity' of the therapist and the idea that the therapist knows what is best for the client: 'The problem with this view, however, is that the notion of a truly scientific investigator, observer or experimenter has been sufficiently cast into doubt by developments within science itself' (p. 248). He further points out the dangers of the therapist's authority with regard to giving the therapist 'unnecessary and potentially abusive power'. Starhawk emphasises the dangers inherent in the therapist's authority:

> Healing that empowers and liberates springs from a mutual struggle with the forces that hurt us all. When we start believing we are 'more together' than someone else, we use our healing power as another way to establish our own superiority. (1987, p. 147)

The client's acceptance of the therapist's authority is seen as a necessary prerequisite for CBT, and when a client disagrees with the model or does not comply with requests, this is seen as a 'setback', or indeed as an opportunity to challenge the client's thoughts and beliefs. This demonstrates the *power outcomes* (Cromwell and Olson, 1975; see Chapter 1), i.e. who has the final say in decisions, which is clearly the therapist. From the beginning, CBT is presented as the right way to think; success occurs when the client thinks and behaves in accordance with the CBT model. If therapy fails, it is because the client has not followed the therapist's suggestions sufficiently; the responsibility is with the client. As Spinelli explains, because of the therapist's unquestioning belief in the principles and assumptions underlying the CBT model, therapeutic failure can 'be blamed on . . . the client's misapplication of (or unwillingness to apply) the specified instructions presented by the therapist' (1994, p. 244).

Social control
Spinelli (1994) points out that the therapist makes judgements about what is rational or desirable, and that these judgements are culturally influenced, culturally desirable. One example of this is the appeal to the rationality of science, clearly a value held by mainstream culture. He explains that,

> In this way, the therapist becomes a broadly libertarian representative of the norms and codes of conduct of society in which both the therapist and client are members. (p. 249)

However, he points out that these cultural norms are not 'objective', and that, in pretending to be objective, cognitive behavioural therapists 'run the risk of imposing a socially conformist ideology on the client' (p. 249). Here Spinelli also points to the dangers of therapists justifying values with respect to science and claiming 'objectivity'. Pilgrim and Treacher similarly explain:

> Psychologists . . . could play out a highly political role in terms of the management of the population, whilst at the same time disowning such a role by pointing to their 'disinterested' scientific training and credentials. (1992, p. 30)

This is particularly relevant to the ignoring, in CBT, of the social structural positions and material realities of oppression and power; the focus on changing the thinking of the individual rather than on the material realities of people's lives.

Spinelli's critique is from a structural framework of power. It is assumed that objectivity gives authority and power to the therapist, authority and power being synonymous with power as a possession. Power is seen to be unidirectional and oppressive. The critique of science, however, fits in much more with a Foucaultian perspective on power (see Chapter 4), i.e. with the relationship between power and knowledge and the role of normative rules in constituting subjects. It is clear that the explicit aim in CBT is to reconstitute the subjectivity of the client; to change the way the client thinks about the world. Thus, it seems that Foucault's 'practices of the self' are an integral part of what happens in therapy. Theory in CBT is a normalising discourse. From Foucault's later work, this describes the dynamic nature of power, where individuals constitute (create) themselves within the context of the normative rules, the disciplinary techniques of the self. These regulative practices are explicit within CBT, where the normative rules of how clients should reconstitute themselves are spelt out.

It is also clear from Foucault's consideration of the practices of the self that clients too have a role in resisting and constituting themselves within the context of these normative rules. However, as McNay (1992) points out in her critique of Foucault, by not prioritising how different techniques of the self are imposed to different levels, Foucault's notions of the subject's agency and the idea of aesthetic stylisation of the self hide the force of cultural norms (see Chapter 4). The issue here concerns how much the therapists uses their authority to enforce the norms established by CBT. Do clients have a choice to constitute themselves in their own way, or is the choice only to take on the idea and norms of CBT wholeheartedly or leave therapy? Given also that clients will seek therapy when in a state of distress, their choices or resistance to the norms communicated by the therapist are likely to be very limited. Thus, it may be more realistic to talk about Foucault's concept of disciplinary power as he applied it to the human sciences (see Chapter 4), while acknowledging a limited role for the client in terms of resistance.

In addition, the goals of CBT fit in with the description by Deleuze and Guattari (1984) of psychic repression, namely, to quell strong emotions and replace them with 'rationality'. Deleuze and Guattari argue that psychic repression is a mechanism to achieve social repression and control, so again, CBT could be said to be used as an agent of social control.

The 'collaborative' relationship

The style of therapy is described as 'collaborative empiricism' (Beck et al., 1979). The joint nature of the therapeutic relationship is emphasised. Kirk clarifies the nature of this 'collaboration', saying:

> The collaborative nature of the therapeutic relationship should be discussed; the patient is expected to participate actively by collecting information, giving feedback on the effectiveness of techniques, and making suggestions about new strategies. (Kirk, 1989, p. 14)

The therapist is expected to structure sessions and use reinforcement selectively to encourage the patient to talk more about what the therapist considers most relevant and most likely to promote change. This would refer to a *power process* (Cromwell and Olson, 1975) — an interactional technique to take control over an aspect of the relationship (see Chapter 1). Therapists are to explain to their patients that talking about how problems are *now* is most useful, as CBT focuses on the immediate circumstances.

Thus, it is clear that the 'collaborative' relationship emphasises the therapist's expectations of the client, that the client will contribute to the therapist's ideas and plans for treatment (within the CBT model). While some things are perhaps negotiable, there are clearly some aspects of CBT that the patient must agree to for the therapy to go ahead. It is clear that the therapist structures the sessions and decides what is useful for the client to talk about. Thus, the idea of collaboration seems to incorporate a demand that the client will conform to and welcome the therapist's approach and will agree to various forms of activity that the therapist suggests.

'Collaboration', but different roles

Turnbull suggests that this is not collaboration between equals:

> It is better to see the client and therapist occupying different roles but collaborating on a joint enterprise. The therapist's role in the relationship is to make decisions concerning therapy and the client's role is to take decisions about how this can be applied to his or her lifestyle. In order to work properly, this collaboration needs to be based on a mutual respect for each other's role. (1996, p. 20)

Turnbull cites Rogers' core conditions as key qualities of a therapist, which will help develop trust and encourage collaboration. He suggests that these conditions should be used to encourage compliance in the client. Here the notion of collaboration and compliance are used interchangeably. He also points out an aspect of the cognitive behaviour therapist's power with respect to the client: that of the therapist's authority and 'superior knowledge' (p. 20). He contends that the client must accept the therapist's superior knowledge, although not to the extent where the client's ability to self-manage is compromised. How to achieve this balance is not explained. In short, 'There are times when the authority of a therapist's knowledge must be exercised and accepted by the client' (p. 20). Thus, for Turnbull it is important that the client accept the cognitive behaviour therapist as the one with the knowledge, and hence the decision-maker with regard to the therapy. Again, it is explicit that the therapist is the one with the final say, an analysis of *power outcomes* (Cromwell and Olson, 1975; see Chapter 1) clearly demonstrating the extent of the power of the therapist in CBT. Here the connection between power and knowledge is explicit.

Control

Marshall (1996) describes the aim of CBT as helping clients take control of their problems and deal with future problems in an 'adaptive' way. She stresses:

> In all these areas the aim is the same, that is, for the person to manage their lives adaptively by recognising the interaction between thoughts, feelings and behaviours. (p. 32)

Thus, the role of the cognitive behaviour therapist is to educate the client with regard to this interaction. Marshall points out that the therapist's control should be minimal by the end of therapy and that 'during therapy the amount of control individuals accept for themselves will vary' (p. 32). However, she predicts that initially the therapist will direct therapy and that as time goes on the client, in collaboration with the therapist, will direct the therapy. Here the terminology used clearly indicates that it is the client's responsibility to take control, the implication being that it is the client's fault if they do not take control. There seems to be no responsibility given to the therapist for their part in this or for how they may influence the client's behaviour.

Critique of the notion of 'collaboration'

Lowe (1999) criticizes the notion of 'collaboration' as an appeal to promote equality, which, he argues, is impossible in the context of therapy and the power embedded in the institutional role of the therapist. He explains:

> How collaborative can collaboration be . . . if . . . institutionalised within a particular mode of practice? It is one thing to offer clients a voice within a professional therapeutic discourse, but it might be quite another thing to allow them a discourse of their own. (p. 82)

He further points to the effects of these discourses with respect to power: in fact, to increase the power of the therapist, by concealing it:

> Though the declarative intent of these ideas may be to empower clients, the constitutive effects might be quite the opposite, being not so much disempowering but what Potter . . . calls mis-empowering: adding new tools to the armoury of the already powerful. (p. 83)

Thus, he demonstrates how the rhetoric of 'collaboration' can actually increase the power of the therapist and hide the power imbalance between therapist and client.

Telford and Farrington (1996) usefully point to the dangers within CBT of the rhetoric of 'collaboration' and 'equality' in the therapy relationship, to obscure the power differential between client and therapist that does remain. They also suggest ways in which the therapeutic relationship can be used to help clients take more control over their own therapy. They give an example where the therapist avoids suggesting solutions to the client but instead 'guides' the client to find their own solutions. However, this seems to reflect a one-dimensional understanding of power (as described by Lukes, 1974; see Chapter 3), and a level of the therapist's power is still being missed here. The therapist 'guiding' the client to what the therapist believes will be a good solution means that the therapist is shaping the outcome of the client's decisions. Ultimately, it seems that the client is encouraged to take control over their own therapy as long as they do it following the therapist's model and ideas — almost a situation of 'you can make the decision as long as you decide what I think is good for you'. At the same time, the therapist is encouraged to use their power to increase the client's compliance with CBT. Thus, the therapist's authority is not really questioned or problematised.

The notion of 'collaboration' seems to appeal to a notion of reducing power imbalances in therapy. However, the notion of power implied by this is a one-dimensional view of power. Collaboration is achieved when the client agrees and complies with the therapist's worldview. The notion of collaboration seems to be very muddled with the idea of compliance in CBT. However, as Gramsci points out (Ransome, 1992; see Chapter 3), there is a distinction between coercive and consensual control, and power is still involved in consensual control. There are further dimensions of power (as suggested by Lukes, 1974; again, see Chapter 3) that are missed from the account of collaboration. The extent to which the therapist determines what can be put on the agenda to talk about, or how much the client has been shaped to know what the therapist does not want to hear about, is not considered. It is also clear that the therapist is seen to have authority about what is best for the client, authority that is legitimised by the therapist's knowledge of science. This notion of legitimation of power through science follows clearly in the tradition of Hobbes and Weber (as described in Chapter 3).

It would be more honest and accurate to refer to *compliance* rather than 'collaboration', and thus be explicit about the nature of power relations involved.

The therapy relationship in CBT: the 'therapeutic alliance'
Farrington and Telford (1996) consider the therapeutic relationship in CBT and emphasise the importance of the client trusting the therapist, both for the client to feel comfortable enough to disclose openly and for the client to be more likely to act on the advice of the therapist. They cite Schaap et al.'s (1993) finding that clients are less likely to comply with treatment if the therapist is too domineering and controlling, too rejecting of the client's views or in complete disagreement with the client's views. They also examine the factors of the client's perception of the therapist's expertise and credibility, and suggest ways to improve this. They consider

that warmth and empathy displayed by the therapist are important but not sufficient for positive therapeutic change. They point to Schaap et al.'s (1993) observation of the scant regard that CBT has paid to the therapeutic relationship or to 'non-specific' factors in therapy and suggest that research concerning the nature of the 'therapeutic alliance' in CBT would be useful. The confusion in terms here, using the terminology of 'therapeutic alliance' from psychoanalytic therapy while considering the core conditions from person-centred therapy in relation to CBT, is an example of the lack of clarity and consideration of the therapy relationship within CBT.

The focus seems to be that the importance of this 'therapeutic alliance' lies in increasing the client's compliance with or belief in the therapist, and therefore the power of the therapist to influence the client. The aim is to achieve these ends through the relationship rather than to achieve meaning within the relationship. Spinelli highlights this emphasis, explaining that,

> While there is some acknowledgement of the significance of the relationship between client and therapist, nevertheless its importance tends to be stressed as a means to an end (which is the client's willingness to learn from the therapist and apply the learning-based goals that have been set) rather than being of value in and of itself. (1994, p. 251)

Thus, the idea of the alliance in CBT seems to be about how much the client accepts the therapist's authority and complies with the therapist's requests.

Rogers' core conditions

Marshall (1996) looks in detail at the therapeutic relationship in CBT. She identifies Rogers' core conditions (see Chapter 6) and expands on the meaning of these for cognitive behaviour therapists. She stresses the importance of empathy, meaning that the therapist should try and understand the client's formulation of their problem and particularly must not challenge how the client says (s)he feels. Marshall also points out that, while aiming to accurately empathise with a client's problem, the cognitive behaviour therapist will be reframing and reinterpreting the client's problem. No comment is made about the incompatibility of these goals. Empathy is merely suggested as a way in which the therapist can encourage the client to feel more positive towards the therapist and therefore be more likely to accept the therapist's reframing and agree to the tasks set — again, a technique used to increase the authority of the therapist. The possibility of the client's not accepting the therapist's understanding of their problem (from their cognitive behavioural framework) is not addressed.

Marshall (1996) then discusses the importance of genuineness, and misuses this concept to underline the importance of the therapist telling the client when they believe the client is behaving or thinking in unhelpful ways, in other words to justify the therapist's challenging the client. She goes on to point out the difficulties of unconditional positive regard for the cognitive behaviour therapist, and suggest that adopting an unquestioning approach could lead to 'a situation where no change is possible because the therapist is not able to challenge their client' (p. 42).

She suggests that in CBT opportunities should be used, when clients express their beliefs (for example that they do not believe the homework set will be useful), to challenge these beliefs and the automatic thoughts involved. It seems that, contrary to the principles of unconditional positive regard and empathy, clients' beliefs are there to be challenged. Thus, Marshall (1996) concludes that Rogers' core conditions have limited applicability to CBT. In fact, unconditional positive regard and empathy are incompatible with the challenging beliefs involved in CBT. However, no alternative framework for focusing on the therapy relationship is presented. Instead, the therapist's authority and expert role are emphasised.

Burns and Auerbach (1996) further examine the role of empathy in CBT. They cite research investigating the link between therapist empathy and therapeutic outcome and conclude that:

> The patients of therapists who were the warmest and most empathic improved significantly and substantially more than the patients of therapists with the lowest empathy ratings, even when controlling for other factors. This indicates that even in a highly technical form of therapy such as CBT, the quality of the relationship has a substantial impact on the degree of clinical recovery. (p. 144)

They suggest that CBT training may have an adverse effect on therapists' ability to be empathic, pointing out that empathy 'requires a sudden paradigm shift that may be confusing for some cognitive therapists' (p. 149). Furthermore, 'Technical and empathic interventions require dramatically different types of therapeutic and personal aptitudes' (p. 150). They suggest that the times when therapists particularly need to switch to an empathic mode of responding are when the patient expresses anger or distrust towards the therapist, or when the patient is upset or needs to ventilate. However, Burns and Auerbach point out that therapists' belief in the CBT model can lead them to dismiss the client's criticism as unreasonable and to be challenged.

Here they seem to be suggesting that empathy is important in its own right, rather than just as a means to an end. They also seem to be acknowledging that there is the potential for the therapist to take too much control, and that this is not beneficial. The implicit message seems to be that there is an optimum amount of control for the therapist to take; the therapist is clearly the expert in authority, but the client also should be given some say and some understanding of their position. In addition,

Burns and Auerbach seem to be making some acknowledgement of the power of the client to agree with the therapist or to resist the therapist's power, and to be suggesting empathy as a means of preventing the client's resistance. Here there would appear to be a move away from a structural model of power, possessed by the therapist and held over a powerless client, towards a suggestion that power is dynamic in the therapy relationship.

Telford and Farrington (1996) stress that it is vital for CBT to accept the importance of the therapy relationship:

> Cognitive behaviourists must wake up to the fact that the notion of the therapist as a neutral onlooker is no longer acceptable within therapy and develop their research strategy to include process as well as product research. (p. 149)

Here, there is some acknowledgement that 'objectivity' has been called into question, and the possibility of a therapist being a neutral scientist whose values are not involved is a dangerous one. However, the full implications of this problematising of objectivity are not developed, with respect to either the knowledge base of CBT or the therapist's position in the relationship. The inconsistencies in the questioning yet acceptance of the authority of the therapist are again not explored.

Ethics

Allison (1996) discusses an ethical framework for CBT. She points out that

> It would be easy to ignore or undervalue the ethical dilemmas involved in the delivery of CBT. After all, is it not true that all CBT interventions are aimed at improving life for the sufferer who is consulting you? How can such well-motivated intentions be ethically doubtful? (p. 156)

The clear lack of concern with the therapist's self-awareness implied by this last statement is in accord with the lack of emphasis on self-awareness for the cognitive behavioural therapist. The question also implies the model's belief that the therapist is the one with answers that clearly apply to all clients, as science has demonstrated. The unquestioned assumption of the expert and objective therapist is demonstrated in the CBT literature by the lack of references to ethics or power.

Allison emphasises that cognitive behaviour therapists are involved in promoting change, and that the changes may well bring about less desirable consequences, sometimes predictable and at other times not. She summarises the implications of this by saying

> In common with other treatment modalities, CBT will sometimes be successful, sometimes not so successful and sometimes [will]

have unplanned for side-effects. Because CBT interventions have enormous potential for bringing about change it is perhaps arguably even more important that interventions are designed in an ethically sound form. (1996, p. 158)

Here, she points to the explicit aim of CBT to change the client, to change the way they view the world and think about themselves. This assumes the idea of a stable unitary self, rather than a self that is constantly being reconstituted in relationships, as Foucault would postulate (see Chapter 4). However, it is also clear from this how much the aim of CBT is to reconstitute the subjectivity of the client. Even if it is accepted that individuals constantly reconstitute themselves in relationships, the therapy relationship is one in which the authority of the therapist provides a different context with respect to power and their influence on the reconstitution of the client. She notes the dangers of CBT with regard to side-effects or not-so-successful treatment outcomes, which would seem to be an acknowledgement of the limitations of the applicability of science and research findings to unique individuals. In addition, the terminology demonstrates how much the model of CBT as a treatment fits with a medical model of distress.[1] However, this does not mean that she questions the authority of the therapist, which is based on the rationality and knowledge of science.

Ethical principles
Allison (1996) also points to the influence of the individual's belief systems and worldview, as influenced by gender and class, on making ethical decisions. She considers the four principles to guide ethical decisions used in models of medical ethics: respect for autonomy, beneficence, non-maleficence, and justice. In examining how each of these principles applies to CBT, she notes that in the early stages of CBT the therapist will lead the planning of the care programme. The justification for this is that 'the client at that time does not have a clear idea of where she most needs help or, indeed, what help she needs' (pp. 159–60). No reference is made to clients who do have a clear idea of what help they may need, or even just a clear idea of what they would not find helpful. Here, with no regard to the autonomy of the client, beneficence is justified to be the guiding ethical principle by the educational metaphor of therapy, and the client is relegated to the role of ignorant pupil. Allison points out that decisions made by the therapist at this time encroach on the autonomy of the client, 'particularly where compliance is expected and where little, if any, contribution is being made by the client at that point in treatment' (p.

1. The CBT alliance with the medical model is very important in terms of the wider context of psychiatry and the power in this institution, particularly of drug companies, which fund much of the research on CBT. There is a vested interest among CBT researchers seeking funding to produce research that complements the medical model rather than challenges it; hence the number of papers on CBT that recommend it as a 'useful adjunct to medication'.

160). She stresses the importance of informed consent at this point and recommends that coercion be outlawed. No reference is made to power inherent in consensual as well as coercive control (see Gramsci, Chapter 3). This seems to be justified again by appeal to the scientific knowledge of the therapist.

Beneficence and non-maleficence are two principles that Allison (1996) suggests need to be balanced. She acknowledges that some aspects of a CBT programme may be unpleasant or frightening for a client, but says that they need to be balanced by the greater good that could be the aim of the exercise. However, she does exercise a word of caution about therapists making these decisions with respect to the threat of the client's autonomy:

> Basing decisions on the foundation that you are exercising your judgement in order to bring about a better outcome for the client may well be a paternalistic way of working and may subjugate the client's autonomy to the therapist's power. (p. 160)

However, there are no suggestions for how to avoid subjugating the client's autonomy in CBT.

Client's autonomy or therapist's authority?

In applying an ethical framework to CBT, Allison (1996) points out the particular inconsistency between the principle of respecting the autonomy of the client and CBT. She explains:

> In order to truly respect the autonomy of the client, it is necessary to accept the person unconditionally. This means to respect the other person as an equal, without censure or judgement. Clients generally become clients because they have a need, which can be met (at least theoretically!) by the therapist. This immediately puts the client in a position of dependency. As a result, the client finds themselves with little choice but to place their trust in a professional. (p. 166)

The principles and beliefs that underlie the practice of CBT are that the cognitive behaviour therapist has information and a framework for understanding the client's problems, which the client does not have at the beginning of therapy. Thus, the therapist is believed to be in a better position to decide what the client needs. There is little consideration given to the dangers of the power inherent in the beneficent CBT therapist's position. It is suggested that part of CBT entails giving the client the information about the model to enable self-understanding and autonomous decision-making. However, it is not clear at what point the client's autonomy is considered, particularly if the client does not agree with what the therapist believes to be best. Respecting the client's autonomy in CBT is directly opposed by the belief that the therapist has rationality and science on their side and therefore knows what is best for the client, whatever the client may believe. Ultimately, with the model of the therapist as superior, the client's views can be dismissed as 'irrational' by an appeal to science which could be hard for a client to argue with, given the authority that science still has in this culture.

Paternalism

Turnbull (1996) discusses in more detail paternalism in the therapy relationship in CBT. He suggests that CBT can be paternalistic particularly in the early stages of a relationship, where the therapist

> May sometimes need to coerce the client into carrying out actions which he or she will find unpleasant in order that progress can ultimately be made. This is something that may often be required early in therapy when the client may not be in a position to make choices. (Turnbull, 1996, p. 19)

Turnbull defends this type of coercion by stating that it should be based on the ethical principles of beneficence, but he admits that this must be acknowledged as an example of paternalism. He does not explain why, at the start of therapy, a client may not be in a position to make choices, and does not seem to consider the alternative of providing clients with the necessary information to enable them to make a choice. Compliance seems to be sought in preference to informed consent, and no comments are made about the dangers of the therapist justifying coercion by beneficence, or the possibility of the therapist *not* being in a position to know the client's best interests. There seems to be no question that the therapist's knowledge of the model and the scientific principles behind CBT put the therapist in a position to know what is best for the client.

Paternalism or autonomy?

Searle (1993) discusses ethical dilemmas in therapy and the competing values of paternalism or autonomy. She suggests that moral justification for the teleological principle of beneficence is sought from the outcome. She argues that this ethical principle is often used to defend paternalism. Beneficence is used to protect the client from autonomy when this could result in harm, or even just when the therapist does not agree with a client's decision and believes they know best. She describes the competing deontological principle of autonomy, which suggests that the therapist has a duty to respect the integrity and individuality of the client and must therefore respect their autonomy. She asserts that the values of the therapist influence therapy in many ways, particularly because of the power difference in the therapy relationship. She suggests that it is essential that clients make their own choices regarding values, and that being exposed to the therapist's value system should be an issue for informed consent.

In CBT, therapists are encouraged to express their values and beliefs in the cognitive model as the 'right' values and beliefs. *Informed consent* is often ignored in favour of coercion, and autonomy rejected in favour of beneficence, thus increasing the power of the therapist. The principle of beneficence also seems to be justified by the belief that the outcome of a client's changing their thinking in accordance with CBT principles is inevitably good and beneficial to the client. The risk of whether a particular client may not believe that the ends justify the means is not considered. This again is a result of the appeal to research and science, which then concludes that CBT is right for everybody, despite research demonstrating that CBT helps less than 100% of its clients. The conviction that one way of thinking is the answer for everyone is directly opposed to having respect for the autonomy of each individual client.

Allison (1996) finally argues that ethical principles are particularly important in CBT where the therapist may make decisions for a client in the client's best interests if their autonomy is thought to be impaired by their emotional suffering. She claims that recourse to principles and independent criteria is essential for the therapist to judge what is in the client's best interests. However, it is not clear how these principles are to be used when considering such interests, when the principle of autonomy has been rejected. She concludes with a reiteration of the importance of clinical supervision, of the need to explore ethics and encourage professional growth, and to demonstrate the value placed in CBT of responsibility and accountability. It seems likely, however, that this simply amounts to another appeal to science and research findings concerning CBT, as there do not seem to be any obvious independent criteria regarding an individual client. It may be that Allison is referring to ethical principles, or perhaps to independent criteria concerning an individual from others who know the client well or from clinical supervision. However, this is not elaborated on any further with respect to how the therapist can claim to know what is best for the client without relying on an appeal to science. Any other principles are notably absent.

Power-from-within of the client
The rhetoric of 'collaboration' in CBT seems to imply the importance of the '*power-from-within*' of the client (see Chapter 3). Telford and Farrington refer to the client's power, saying

> If therapy is successful, it must help the client to assume his/her own power, in other words to become his/her own therapist. Thus if the client is to generalise his/her gains and self-maintain, the balance of perceived power must shift from being invested (by the client) in the therapist to being invested in the client him/herself. (1996, p. 125)

Here the concept of power used by them is implicitly one in which power (seen as a possession) passes from the therapist to the client, although the power is always over the client's life. There seems to be a conflation of two models of power, one of which concerns domination and power over someone ('*power-over*'), which the therapist initially has over the client. Then the client should become empowered through the therapist. This seems to be another model of power, an internal individual notion of power, or Starhawk's (1987) notion of '*power-from-within*'. The idea of passing power from the therapist to the client also seems to suggest that the therapist initially has power over the client and the client gradually resists this power, the goal of therapy being the abolition of the therapist's domination. It is not clear, however, how this resistance or process is supported or encouraged by the behaviour of the therapist. The goal of therapy to encourage the client's '*power-from-within*' is not consistent with the means of the therapist's '*power-over*' the client.

Self-regulation
This concept of power assumes a behavioural, one-dimensional concept of power, visible only when the therapist dominates and controls the therapy by their instructions. Implicit in the writing about CBT is the notion that therapy is successful when clients take on the CBT model and the worldview of the therapist, i.e. when the clients begin to regulate and discipline themselves in line with the therapist's ideas (see Chapter 4 and Foucault's notion of disciplinary power). Thus, even when clients begin to make their own decisions and are seen to be acquiring their own power, it could be argued that this reflects their internalisation of the norms suggested by the therapist. The clients have begun to regulate themselves, with no further need for the therapist to encourage this. This idea is reminiscent of Foucault's reference to Bentham's Panoptican,[2] when surveillance starts to be conducted individually by those being surveyed. Here, clients take over the therapist's role and become surveyors and regulators of their own thoughts. However, this does not remove the power in the norms internalised by the client, or the power of the therapist in communicating and encouraging these norms to be internalised.

Power in personal histories (*historical power*)

It could be claimed that the intention behind CBT — to change the negative automatic thoughts and negative schema of the client — could be to increase the internal feeling of '*power-from-within*' in the client and reduce the power of clients' personal histories of powerlessness. However, the means by which CBT attempts to achieve this is not consistent with the ends. It is difficult to argue that the aim of CBT is to increase the power of the client, by the therapist using '*power-over*' or their authority. However, here there lies a possibility in how CBT techniques could be used

---

2. In Foucault (1977), *Discipline and Punish*.

differently, by a client who knowingly chooses to use the techniques to reduce the power of previously internalised 'negative schema' without a mandate to replace them with what the therapist judges more helpful. In this way, challenging negative thoughts could be used by clients as a means of resisting domination by others and questioning previously taken-for-granted assumptions about themselves. However, this would need to be clearly led by the client, with no suggestion from the therapist about how to replace these thoughts with new internalised prescriptions.

Structural social power (*societal power*)

CBT theory takes no account of issues of power arising from social structural positions. There is a danger that, in challenging the 'realism' of client's thoughts, material realities of power are ignored and deemed 'unrealistic'. Johnstone (1989) criticises cognitive approaches for locating the problem within the individual, following the medical model. She points out that

> There is a danger of conceptualising treatment as a kind of fixing of
> a faulty machine, while the rigid barrier between 'mad' and 'sane'
> (or in its cognitive version between 'rational' and 'irrational') is
> maintained. (p. 90)

She suggests that cognitive therapy needs to understand problems within a personal and wider context and therefore to work towards change at a 'whole-person, whole-system level, not just a cognitive one' (p. 90).

Similarly, Smail (1987) criticises cognitive therapy for attempting to 'juggle your cognitions'. He suggests that the task of therapy should be to help people to make life more bearable, which he suggests is 'far preferable to collaborating in the construction of a web of social deceit'; in other words, he is saying that the reality of people's lives cannot be changed by thinking about them differently. Further,

> Chaos, eccentricity and pain are among the inevitable ingredients
> of everybody's experience; our aim should be neither to tame them
> nor fear them, nor even try to soothe them, but rather to support
> the individual as he or she tries to understand and make use of them.
> (p. 401)

Summary and conclusion

Very little attention is paid to the issue of power in most literature on CBT. The majority of references to the therapy relationship are from one text (Marshall and Turnbull, 1996). Yet CBT invests much authority in therapists who, according to the model, know what is best for their client. There are few considerations of the dangers of this position, and little questioning of the assumptions behind it. The lack of consideration of power in the CBT therapy relationship is not surprising, given that there is very little theorisation of this relationship within CBT, or questioning of the rationality and objectivity of science.

I have discussed the concept of 'collaboration', which can be used to obscure the power differential in CBT. 'Collaboration' seems to refer to the importance of the client's compliance with the therapist's requests and acceptance of the therapist's expert power. From a Foucaultian perspective, collaboration could also refer to the client's internalisation of the norms established by the therapists concerning the 'right' or 'helpful' way to think.

I have also considered the competing ethical principles of autonomy and beneficence. At least at the start of a CBT relationship, beneficence takes priority at the expense of the client's autonomy. At this point it is assumed that the therapist is in the best position to decide what is in the client's best interests, and the basis for the therapist's knowledge is not questioned, but is justified by the legitimising function of science.

There is very little mention of the pitfalls or dangers of the therapist's deciding what is best for the client, and of their assumption of neutrality or objectivity. However, Allison (1996) does mention the importance of the therapist's self-awareness and the need for clinical supervision to try and ensure that the therapists are using their power to benefit the client and not to fulfil their own needs. Given the philosophy of the CBT model, however, it is not apparent how a focus on self-awareness in supervision could be accommodated (and it is certainly not theorised as being part of the model). This would be particularly relevant if supervision were a process by which the therapist and supervisor joined forces to decide what was in the best interests of the client.

There seem to be two discourses relevant to the issue of power in CBT. The first is that of 'collaboration', and the importance of the client's actively being involved in the process. However, this notion often obscures the nature of this collaboration, which concerns the client's agreeing with the therapist and obscures the power inherent in the relationship. Simultaneously, the discourse of collaboration is also delegitimised by the model of the 'expert' therapist who knows what is best for the client. Here, power and authority are acknowledged and are seen as necessary and positive. It is suggested that it is necessary to persuade the client to do what the therapist thinks is best, and to this end the therapist's authority is used in the client's best interests. Science and rationality as an arbitrator and decider of an individual's best interests are unquestioned.

It is necessary for CBT to look realistically and honestly at the dynamics of power in therapy relationships. Without this, CBT therapists are in danger of obscuring their power and not taking an ethical stance to avoid domination and abuse.

Chapter 6

Person-Centred Therapy: equality in the therapy relationship?

In this chapter, I consider Carl Rogers' emphasis on the importance of issues of power in the therapy relationship. Rogers challenged the power inherent in the role of the therapist in many revolutionary ways. Rogers' person-centred theory is based on the principle of respect for each individual and their autonomy. It is a radical theory of therapy and is heretical to psychiatric understanding of mental illness. The theory of psychological distress is based on internalised oppression, and the effect of person-centred therapy is to reduce the power that others have had over clients and thus increase their own sense of personal power, or '*power-from-within*' (see Chapter 3). In his later work, Rogers also focused on the structural power in society, and I suggest that to consider all aspects of power fully, the person-centred therapist needs to consider the 'socially positioned individual' (Kearney, 1996). In this chapter, I illustrate person-centred theory through my experience as a client with a person-centred therapist.

Person-centred theory

Person-centred therapy (PCT) was first described by Carl Rogers in the 1950s and was elaborated by him until his death in 1987. Rogers was a psychologist. He developed this way of being with patients (whom he called 'clients') and called it 'counselling', as he was forbidden to use the word 'therapy' because of his lack of medical training. There has been much research evidence supporting the efficacy of person-centred or client-centred therapy for clients with many different types of difficulties, including psychotic experiences. The theories behind the therapy have been developed by Rogers and others to inform a 'person-centred approach' which can be used in various settings, including education, the workplace and in the resolution of international conflict.

The philosophy of PCT is founded on a belief in the innate potential for constructive growth in each individual, which Rogers termed the 'actualising tendency' (Rogers, 1959). He believed in the potential of each living organism to grow to the best of its ability and of humans to grow towards their potential, which is constructive both for each individual and for society as a whole. He hypothesised that this actualising tendency can be thwarted (although never killed completely until the organism dies) by conditions in the environment, specifically when the individual encounters *conditions of worth*. Conditions of worth are messages that individuals are acceptable only if they think, feel or behave in a certain way. If people receive conditions of worth, they begin to internalise these conditions as a self-concept of what they 'should' be, which, over time, can lead the individual to become further and further removed from the 'organismic self' (Rogers' term for the experiencing self within). This discrepancy between the self-concept and the organismic self, and the ways that individuals have for coping with this, is hypothesised to be the cause of psychological distress.

Rogers asserted that 'facilitative conditions' need to be provided to help the self-actualising tendency fulfil its full potential and work as well as possible. He describes these facilitative conditions in Rogers 1959. They were derived from research to investigate what was helpful for clients in therapy. He explains:

> For therapy to occur, it is necessary that these conditions exist:
> 1) That two persons are in contact.
> 2) That the first person, whom we shall term the client, is in a state of *incongruence*, being *vulnerable* or *anxious*.
> 3) That the second person, whom we shall term the therapist, is *congruent* in the *relationship*.
> 4) That the therapist is *experiencing unconditional positive regard* toward the client.
> 5) That the therapist is *experiencing* an *empathic* understanding of the client's *internal frame of reference*.
> 6) That the client *perceives*, at least to a minimal degree, conditions 4 and 5, the *unconditional positive regard* of the therapist for him, and the *empathic* understanding of the therapist. (Cited in Kirschenbaum and Henderson, 1989, p. 213, original emphasis)

Rogers (1957) describes these conditions similarly in his 'integration statement' (Bozarth, 1998), where he asserts that they are the necessary and sufficient conditions in all therapy.

Rogers further clarifies that, as the precondition for the other conditions to be fulfilled, it is necessary for two persons to be in *contact* (the first condition above). He explains psychological contact as that in which 'each makes some perceived difference in the experiential field of the other' (1957, cited in Kirschenbaum and Henderson, 1989, p. 221). In the second condition, the state of incongruence refers to the discrepancy between the self-concept and the organismic self. The third condition requires that the therapist be congruent or integrated. While Rogers points out that no one individual can be fully integrated at all times, he is referring to the time of the therapy contact:

> It is enough if in this particular moment of this immediate relationship with this specific person he is completely and fully himself, with his experience of the moment being accurately symbolised and integrated into the picture he holds of himself. (ibid, p. 215)

The therapist must be aware of his own inner experiencing and must not be presenting a façade. Rogers also clarifies that congruence means an *awareness* of feelings, and not necessarily communicating these overtly to the client.

Rogers explains that to empathically understand is to sense the client's private world as if it were the therapist's own world. In the final condition above, the client must be able to perceive some acceptance and empathy from the therapist. Rogers again emphasises that the extent to which the conditions (2) to (6) are fulfilled varies, and he hypothesises that, the more these conditions are fulfilled, the more the process of therapy will occur. This suggests that these are conditions to be aimed for by therapists and are not suggested as absolutes. Rogers also claims that these are the necessary and sufficient conditions to work with *any* individual, no matter what problems they may have. He asserts that whenever these conditions are met (whether in formal therapy or outside of it) they are similarly effective.

Intrinsic to these facilitative conditions is a non-directive attitude on the part of the therapist. Brodley explains how this attitude follows from the principle of the self-actualising tendency and the facilitative conditions:

> The nondirective attitude . . . influences the therapist to protect the client's self-determined processes that promote the client's self-empowerment. And it fosters the avoidance of therapist intentions and behaviors that might disempower the client. (1997, p. 18)

Rogers (1957) also points out the conclusions that the integration statement forces on the necessity of training for therapists. He asserts that the facilitative conditions are qualities of experience, not intellectual information, and must be acquired through experiential training: formal qualifications are unnecessary for their acquisition. Moreover, a psychological diagnosis or formulation of problems is not necessary for therapy. A further implication of this theory is that 'the techniques of various therapies are relatively unimportant except to the extent that they serve as channels for fulfilling one of the conditions' (cited in Kirschenbaum and Henderson, 1989, p. 233).

Person-centred therapy and power

I have identified three aspects to the power imbalance in the therapy relationship: the power imbalance inherent in roles of 'therapist' and 'client' (*role power*), the personal history of the therapist and particularly the client with respect to the experience of power and powerlessness (*historical power*) and the power distribution with respect to the structural positions in society of the client and therapist (*societal power*) (see Chapter 1).

Power in the role of the therapist (*Role Power*)

The actualising tendency and the non-directive attitude

Rogers explicitly set out to change the role of the therapist from that of an expert and to aim for a more egalitarian therapy relationship. This follows from the philosophy underlying person-centred therapy. Rogers contends that the premise of the actualising tendency challenges the need to control people; i.e. challenges

> The view that the nature of the individual is such that he cannot be trusted — that he must be guided, instructed, rewarded, punished, and controlled by those that are higher in status. (Rogers, 1978a, p. 8)

He explains the implications of this philosophy and values:

> The politics of the person-centred approach is a conscious renunciation and avoidance by the therapist of all control over, or decision-making for, the client. It is the facilitation of self-ownership by the client and the strategies by which this can be achieved; the placing of the locus of decision-making and the responsibility for the effects of these decisions. It is politically centred in the client. (p. 14)

Whereas the belief in the actualising tendency is the foundation of PCT, no injunction follows from this for the therapist to influence the client in a certain direction. Instead, the trust in the client's process leads to the non-directive attitude. The *non-directive attitude* is a way for therapists to express their commitment to avoiding client disempowerment (Brodley, 1997). Rogers (1978a) pointed out the implications of this principle of non-directivity on the part of the therapist by discussing the threat to counsellors of his views: 'I was making it clear that if they agreed with me, it would mean the complete disruption and reversal of their personal control in their counselling relationship' (p. 7). In this sense PCT is a radical disruption of the dynamics of power in therapy. Natiello (2001, p. 11) explains that 'Such a stand is in radical conflict with the prevailing paradigm of authoritarian power.' In my own experience of receiving person-centred therapy, I found the non-directivity on the part of my therapist to be very respectful of my process. It was also important for me to know that I had total control over how I used the time in each session. I needed to know that I would not be led to the issues that my therapist believed were most important, but that I would be followed in whatever direction I chose to take. At the same time, within the attitude of non-directivity, the occasional comment made by my therapist from her frame of reference felt like a gift. I knew that these comments were not intended to influence me or that there was any intention other than my therapist being free to be herself (see Brodley, 1999).

However, others suggest that non-directivity obscures the power of the therapist. Following the critiques of Masson (1989), Pilgrim and Treacher (1992) warn about the dangers of non-directive approaches avoiding issues of power. They assert that

> The new client-centred discourse is to be characterised by one party having more formal knowledge than the other. As psychotherapists have known for years, an approach to professional work which actually minimises authoritative directiveness is, itself, an extremely effective way of having power over clients . . . Non-directiveness and contrived neutrality are themselves evidence of professional power and choice. (p. 164)

The therapist's choice to be non-directive is not a decision to use their power to decide what is best for the client and act accordingly. Instead, in PCT it is a moral principle, the basis being the ethical belief that the client's autonomy should be respected. Grant (1990) claims that the principle of non-directivity can be justified either instrumentally (it helps the client) or morally (for respect for the client). This concept of instrumental non-directiveness (which Grant argues is more relevant to humanistic therapies in general, whereas principled non-directiveness characterises Rogerian person-centred therapy) seems to be what Pilgrim and Treacher (1992) are referring to with respect to the therapist using their power to be non-directive.

Grant emphasises that 'The liberation that can come from client-centred therapy is accomplished by respecting clients as autonomous beings, not by making them autonomous beings' (1990, p. 82). He points to the importance of principled non-directivity as a moral choice to respect the client. He argues that psychotherapy is a moral enterprise and we need to examine the morality of the practices of therapy. He further explains:

> The therapist does not attempt or intend to make anything happen — growth, insight, self-acceptance — in the client, but rather provides the therapeutic conditions in the belief that they are expressions of respect and with the hope that the client will make use of them. (p. 78)

Non-directiveness is not a technique but the expression of the belief in the autonomy of all humans. Grant further clarifies that non-directiveness is not a choice that withholds other ways of being from the client:

> Principled nondirectiveness is an attitude, not a set of behaviours.

> Having the attitude does not mean a stock or a 'hands off' approach to relating to clients, although the most common expression of it is empathic understanding responses . . . Living the attitude means being open and responsive to clients' requests and indications for other types of response . . . Principled nondirect-iveness is an expression of an absence of the *intention* to make anything in particular happen, and of an openness to following the client's direction. (pp. 81–2, original emphasis)

However, it is clear that, for whatever reason (principled or instrumental), the person-centred therapist is making a decision to be non-directive, by making a decision to follow Rogers' theory and be a PCT therapist, and is using the role and authority of the therapist's position to make this choice. This choice should be an issue of informed consent for the client, i.e. the client should be given the information about how the therapist works and the moral principles behind this and should be able to make a choice if they want to work with a particular therapist.

The facilitative conditions
The facilitative conditions all promote and aim for as egalitarian relationship as possible between the therapist and client. Rogers (1978a) examines the therapist core conditions of congruence, unconditional positive regard and empathy with respect to their political implications and the power imbalance between client and therapist. He points out that congruence

> gives a maximum space to be — for the client and the therapist. The therapist is saying, in effect 'Here I am, as I am'. There is no hint of any kind of control over the client's response to her way of being. To the contrary, finding that the therapist is permitting herself to be as she is, the client tends to discover that same freedom. (p. 10)

This was my own experience of therapy as a client. Perceiving my therapist as a person who seemed to feel free to be herself certainly enabled me to feel more comfortable to be *me*. Rogers then discusses the implications of unconditional positive regard and concludes that

> It is a powerful factor, but it is in no way manipulative or controlling in the relationship. There is no judgement or evaluation involved. Power over her own life is left completely in the hands of the client. It provides a nurturant atmosphere but not a forcing one. (1978a, p. 11)

With regard to empathic understanding, Rogers (1978a) argues that it assists the client to gain a clearer understanding of, and hence a greater control over, their own life; i.e. it aims directly to increase the client's personal power. My experience of my therapist trying to understand my internal struggles in a caring and valuing way certainly felt powerful to me, but in a liberating rather than an oppressive way, allowing me to feel freer to be me and to understand and accept myself. I certainly felt that my experience of person-centred therapy increased my feeling of personal power or '*power-from-within*' (see Chapter 1), both in the therapy relationship and in relation to the rest of my life.

Demystification of therapy

Another way in which Rogers addressed the imbalance of power in the therapy relationship was to make person-centred therapy transparent and explicit, to demystify the therapy. He did this by explaining exactly what the therapist does in therapy and providing much tape-recorded and video-recorded material for public use. He placed great importance on the clarity of the process and the content of therapy including the accountability of the therapists to be able to demonstrate the extent to which they fulfilled the core conditions. He similarly demystified the therapist as a person by stressing the concept of congruence.

The demystification of my therapist as a person was a strong factor in my not feeling disempowered in the relationship. It was important for me to know that I could ask her questions about herself if I wanted to, and I did ask her some questions, as I wanted to understand some of her attitudes about life (for example, I asked her why she had married). However, I did not feel the need to ask much about her life, as I found just knowing that I could do so removed the need to a large extent.

A political philosophy

Rogers describes PCT as 'revolutionary' with respect to the political stance and philosophy it upholds: one of his books is entitled *Carl Rogers on Personal Power: Inner Strength and its Revolutionary Impact* (1978a). In discussing the politics of his approach, he defines politics by saying:

> Politics involves the question of where power is located, who makes the choices and decisions, who carries out or enforces those decisions, and who has the knowledge or data regarding the consequences of those decisions. It involves the strategies involved in the taking of power, the distribution of power, the holding of power, and the sharing or relinquishing of power. (Rogers, 1978b, p. 1)

He asserts that opposition to person-centred therapy sprang 'primarily because it struck such an outrageous blow to the therapist's power' (1978b, p. 16). He challenges the notion of expert knowledge which gives power, and believes in the power of congruence, that

> In such an individual, functioning in a unified way, we have the best possible base for wise action. It is a process base, not a static authority base. It is a trustworthiness that does not rest on 'scientific' knowledge. (Rogers, 1978a, p. 250)

Rogers describes in detail his political ideology, the values of which are at the heart of the principles of person-centred therapy:

> I find that for myself I am most satisfied politically:
> 1. When every person is helped to become aware of his or her own power and strength.
> 2. When every person participates fully and responsibly in every decision which effects him or her.
> 3. When group members learn that the sharing of power is more satisfying than endeavouring to use power to control others.
> 4. When the group finds ways of making decisions which accommodate the needs and desires of each person.
> 5. When every member of the group is aware of the consequences of a decision, on its members and on the external world.
> 6. When each person enforces the group decision through self-control of his or her own behaviour.
> 7. When each person feels increasingly empowered, strengthened.
> 8. When each person, and the group as a whole, is flexible, open to change, and regards previous decisions as being always open for consideration. (Rogers, 1978b, p. 2)

Rogers (1978b) also claims that, when a facilitative climate is provided for a group, the members choose to move towards the values and behaviours that he describes. It can be seen that the values are emphasising the constructive growth and power not only of each individual, but of each individual in relation to others in the social context.

Does Rogers make the relationship egalitarian enough?

Few would argue that Rogers made significant steps towards addressing the imbalance of power in therapy. Masson (1989) notes that 'It is unarguable that Rogers did away with some of the "trappings" of the imbalance in the power relationship' (p. 231). He got rid of the idea of the therapist as 'expert', making training more open and less elitist: there is no diagnosis, labelling or manipulation in person-centred therapy. However, Masson remains doubtful that this touched the essential power imbalance in therapy. He seems to be dubious about the possibility of the therapist providing the facilitative conditions. With regard to the concept of empathy, he argues that empathic understanding responses are a form of interpretation, of the therapists adding their own bias to what the clients say. He claims that 'there is no way out of this dilemma. It is the nature of therapy to distort another person's reality' (p. 247). Masson argues that Rogers did not contemplate the possibility that therapists would misunderstand and would not feel unconditional positive regard towards their clients, and that his conditions were idealistic and unrealistic. Furthermore, he contends that Rogers was oblivious to the real conditions of oppression in people's lives. He comments on the lack of 'genuine traumas' in Rogers' case histories, suggesting that Rogers believed that all suffering came from within rather than from conditions in the external world.

Spinelli (1994) addresses some of Masson's (1989) criticisms of person-centred therapy. First of all, he proposes that Masson's critique of the core conditions 'seems to hinge on a desire for perfectionism' (p. 122). He notes that Masson's criticisms rest on a therapist's inability to fulfil the core conditions completely, but goes on to say:

> My own reading would suggest that Rogers sets forward the necessary and sufficient conditions as aims rather than asserting that he — or any other person-centred therapist — has achieved such. (Spinelli, 1994, p. 123)

He further argues that 'Therapy is clearly imperfect, but it is, nevertheless, one of the few ways we have found of confronting certain forms of human misery and pain' (p. 123). From my own experience, my therapist did not understand me perfectly at all times, but what felt important to me was her obvious intention to try her best to understand me as much as she could. It was clear that her intention was not to provide her own interpretation on my life, but to follow my understanding as closely as possible. The result of this for me was to make me feel less alone with my conflicts and pain.

Spinelli further supports that person-centred therapy

> Promotes an egalitarian relationship between therapist and client . . . the therapist is equally free to choose to disclose personal attitudes, feelings or conflicts that arise from the encounter. (1994, p. 257)

He notes this different stance to self-disclosure compared with other models of therapy, and criticises the lack of therapist self-disclosure in most therapy, saying:

> This one-sided stance seems at the very least artificial and unnerving to clients, and it is likely to be the source of a good deal of irritation directed towards the therapist. (Spinelli, 1994, p. 260)

Furthermore, he points out that no self-disclosure can be a further means of maintaining the imbalance of power. While stressing the importance of the method and the purpose of self-disclosure, he also notes that therapists cannot help but self-disclose:

> How they dress, their appearance, their posture, their gestures and mannerisms, the language they employ, their accent, the environmental features of their consulting room, all these factors

and many more 'reveal' them — as, indeed, does the very fact they invest so much significance in their anonymity. (p. 262)

Dangers of forgetting the institutional role power of therapist

However, Masson's doubt that Rogers' changes to the therapy relationship affect the essential imbalance of the therapy relationship may have some validity. Lowe (1999) criticizes this idea of transparency (see Chapter 4) by pointing out that, however transparent, therapy is still institutionalised within a particular mode of practice. Fish (1999) cites Foucault, who also argued against the possibility of 'transparency' in therapy, and claimed that this aim derives from the concept of power as necessarily negative.

As Lowe (1999) notes, claims to make therapy transparent do not remove the inherent power inequality in the roles of therapist and client. However much a therapist does not behave like an expert, the role of the therapist is still there, and the client will always be aware that at any point the therapist *could* choose to use the power in their role. The therapist could of course use the power for the client's benefit; but this notwithstanding, there is still a clear inequality in the positions of therapist and client which is not removed by any kind of therapist behaviour as a person.

Therapist as a person, and in a role

However, Bozarth (1998) considers this argument and cites a discussion between Rogers and Buber in which Buber makes the claim that the therapist-client situation is always unequal. In reply, Rogers argues that this unequal relationship does not accurately describe the therapy relationship. Bozarth quotes Rogers, saying 'This is something immediate, equal, a meeting of two persons on an equal basis, even though, in the world of I-It, it could be seen as a very unequal relationship' (Bozarth, 1998, p. 21). Bozarth suggests that this disagreement is due to the different definitions of power used by Rogers and Buber. He suggests that the person-centred position with regard to power is derived from the view of power from the Latin etymology, *'portiere'*, that essentially means to be all you are capable of being. He suggests that the counter-position seems to focus on the definition of power as 'possession of control, authority, influence over others'. The person-centred concept of power is like Starhawk's (1987) concept of *'power-from-within'* (see Chapter 3). It focuses on power as a positive force, incorporating a respect for others and their individual power. Natiello (2001) describes Rogers' concept of *'personal power'* as

> the ability to act effectively under one's own volition rather than external control. It is a state wherein individuals are acutely aware of and can act upon their own feelings, needs and values. (p.11)

She also suggests that the more 'solid' a therapist's own sense of *'personal power'* is, the less likely they are to control or use '*power-over*' the client. This demonstrates the difference in paradigms of power. With the structural concept of authoritarian power, the more '*power-over*' exercised by the therapist, the less power the client has. However, with the person-centred concept of '*personal power*' or '*power-from-within*', the *more* '*personal power*' felt by the therapist, the more a client is enabled to feel their '*personal power*'. At other times (particularly when talking about groups), this power is seen to be further enhanced by a coming together with others for mutual benefit, using Arendt's concept of power or Starhawk's (1987) idea of '*power-with*' (see Chapter 3).

Burstow (1987) explores in detail the ways in which there is both equality and inequality in the person-centred therapy relationship. She suggests that the therapist and client are equal as humans and in worth and are equally capable of realising their own unique potential. However, she stresses that they are necessarily unequal in their roles; that the therapist is the helper and the client the helpee. She quotes Buber (1970), saying 'there are . . . many I-you relationships which by their very nature may never unfold into complete mutuality if they are to remain faithful to their nature' (Buber, 1970, p. 179). Burstow emphasises that this role of being the helpee necessarily makes the client more vulnerable, although she also stresses the strength that may arise from this vulnerability. She suggests that the danger of asserting equality where it does not exist can be that the vulnerability of the client is missed.

As little domination as possible

Bozarth (1998) continues to suggest that the equality in the person-centred therapy relationship lies 'in the attitude of the therapist's willingness to trust the client to go in his or her direction, way and pace. It is the equality of two individuals in relationship' (p. 21). It is clear that the theoretical and ethical position of the person-centred therapist not to dominate, control or direct the client is paramount to the claims to equality in person-centred theory. Larner (1999) similarly echoes the person-centred view of the revolutionary power of the person-to-person therapy relationship. He claims: 'This stance of being-with-the-other *is* politically empowering, as a human situation where a dialogue of meaning and sharing takes place' (p. 46). Brink (1987) suggests that the objectively real inequality in the therapist-client relationship can be transcended by a felt sense of equality that comes spontaneously when they meet as persons with common humanity. Clearly, the aim of the PCT therapist is explicitly to do as much as possible to avoid dominating the client or constraining the client's elaboration and exploration of themselves.

Danger of ignoring power in therapist's role

However, in focusing on these aspects of the therapist's behaviour, there is a danger that the '*power-over*' (see Chapter 3) inherent in the role of therapist may be missed. It may be that what is understood to be therapeutic in person-centred therapy is the relationship between two people; but one of them is still there in the role of the client, and the other in the role of the therapist. There are different powers in society attached to each of these roles, and this inequality is established in the institution of therapy. It seems that person-centred theory may be emphasising the agency of individuals at the expense of missing the effect of structures of power on individuals. The potential implications for person-centred therapists of ignoring structural power are that they could miss opportunities to help clients from their own position, and they could underestimate or misunderstand the effects on clients' lives of any structures of power. As Larner also emphasises, 'Professional authority, power and social hierarchy in the therapeutic institution are real enough' (1999, p. 49).

Importance of client's perception of therapist

In addition to missing the inequality of power inherent in the roles of therapist and client, the insistence in person-centred theory of talking about an equal relationship in therapy also misses the way the client perceives this relationship. As Starhawk (1987) emphasises, the concept of '*power-with*', and equal consideration being given to all individuals, can work only where each individual has a sense of their inherent value (see Chapter 3). What is important here is not just that the therapist refrains from using '*power-over*' the clients, but also that the clients can believe in and use their own '*power-from-within*'. This is also relevant to the personal history of power and powerlessness of the clients, which will affect how they perceive their own capability to have power in the relationship.

Ethics of an unequal relationship

Larner (1999), instead of emphasising the possibility of therapy being a relationship between equals, stresses the ethical challenge to work within a relationship of unequals. He claims that integral to the ethics needed is a position of humility and of using 'non-power' by the therapist. He proposes a deconstructing therapy, which he claims 'is obliged to be both powerful and non-powerful . . . That therapists can be powerful, but sacrifice themselves for the sake of the other, allows the power of the other to emerge' (p. 41). This concept of being 'non-powerful' seems to refer to the non-directive attitude of the person-centred therapist. Larner further explains:

> Deconstructing psychotherapy is involved in the process of ethical engagement in 'I-thou' relations . . . Therapeutic power is balanced by the ethical stance towards the other, putting the other first before self, recognising others as subjects in their own right. (1999, p. 47)

He refers to Buber's concept of 'I-thou' relations (signified by respect and mutuality), which was also used by Rogers to explain the person-to-person relationship in person-centred therapy. Larner further concurs with person-centred theory saying, 'The therapist does not relate to the client in terms of a theory of the other, but as strangely other' (1999, p. 48). Here he emphasises the respect for the other as a separate and unique being and as the basis of phenomenology, which is core to the person-centred approach. Larner further seems to be commenting on the facilitative conditions in the person-centred approach when he suggests:

> The conscious movement of the therapist towards the other as an ethical stance allows true dialogue of unequals, in which both therapist and client are powerful *and* non-powerful. (1999, p. 48, original italics)

Larner (1999) also emphasises the importance of the therapist's power and the ability to use this ethically. He suggests that the therapist needs to be powerful against violence in the ethical relationship, 'the potential violence of theory, authority, expertise and technology to override the client's contribution to their life narrative' (p. 48). He further suggests that the therapist's power must be used to take a stand against injustice. He claims that 'to not take a position is itself an act of violence, implicitly condoning the injustices suffered by the client' (p. 48). However, it is here that the therapist needs to be most concerned about issues of power in the therapy relationship. In person-centred therapy it should be rare, but it does happen that the therapist communicates something from their own frame of reference (see Brodley, 1999). It is then that there is the greatest potential for the negative effects of the power held by the therapist in the relationship. This is recognised in person-centred theory, but it is also acknowledged that with these communications there is also the potential for the positive use of power. Generally, these comments are the most risky comments that a person-centred therapist will make, and it is important that they are given great consideration and also be considered in clinical supervision.

I was aware sometimes of the power I gave my therapist because of her status and the respect I had for her academically. I noticed that at times this affected my response to her occasional comments from her own frame of reference; for example, I might imbue these comments with a validity and 'truth' that she did not intend, as I discovered when I referred back and tried to clarify my understanding of one of her comments. However, when I perceived these comments as they were intended, they felt almost like gifts from her which reminded me of her wish to avoid '*power-over*' me, but also of her wish not to deny her own '*power-from-within*', which in turn reinforced my perception of my own '*power-from-within*'. This demonstrates the particular issues of power involved when a therapist makes any comments from her own frame of reference, and the possible discrepancy between the therapist's intention in making these comments and how they are perceived by the client.

Despite all the ways in which Rogers attempted to change the power imbalance in therapy, there will always be power attached to the role of therapist in this society. Therapists are given power by institutions and the law, and they have the responsibility of deciding how much they use or abuse that power. There is a danger that person-centred therapists, in focusing on how much they are a 'person' in the therapy relationship and concentrating on '*power-from-within*' and '*power-with*', may forget that they still have a position of authority or '*power-over*' given to them by society. It is also important to remember that clients may always be aware that, however much the therapist has chosen not to act in such a way as to use power over the client, they may choose to at some point in the future.

Personal histories of power and powerlessness (*historical power*)

The process of personality change described by Rogers (1978a) in person-centred therapy directly addresses the second aspect of power regarding personal histories. Rogers found that, as clients experience the facilitative conditions of person-centred therapy, in reciprocity with the conditions provided by the therapist, they begin to listen more acceptantly to themselves; they begin to prize themselves more as the therapist has prized them, and they are able to be more open to their experiencing within. He asserts that, politically,

> By listening to the feelings within, the client reduces the power others have had in inculcating guilts and fears and inhibitions, and is slowly extending the understanding of, and control over, self.
> (1978a, p. 12)

Gradually, the trust of the organismic self increases and the client's personal history of powerlessness (internalised in the self-concept) becomes a less powerful mechanism of disempowerment. Thus, a fortuitous likely impact of the therapist's facilitative conditions is that they are likely to reduce the clients' feelings of disempowerment arising from their personal history.

This was indeed my experience as a client in person-centred therapy. I felt that, as I was understood and accepted, this increased my own self-understanding and self-acceptance, and thus my subjective experience of '*power-from-within*'.

However, the emphasis in person-centred theory on an equal relationship in therapy misses this aspect of power in the therapy relationship — the power in the personal histories of the client and therapist with respect to the experience of power and powerlessness (*historical power*). While Rogers hypothesises that the facilitative conditions will provide a corrective experience for the conditions of worth previously experienced by the client, it is possible it will take some time before the client experiences these conditions as genuine and something to be trusted. This is acknowledged by Rogers' focus on the client's perception of the core conditions. Up to the point where the clients perceive these conditions, the client's perception of the therapist is more likely to be determined by their previous experiences of relationships and their assumptions about therapists. This provides another aspect to the inequality in the therapy relationship, which can be obscured by claims to equality. Even though this inequality is addressed by the provision of the facilitative conditions which increase the clients' sense of '*power-from-within*', therapists need to be aware that, particularly early on in therapy, the clients' perceptions may not be from their inner experiencing and '*power-from-within*' that the therapist wants to encourage.

What I am saying is that there may be a discrepancy between how the therapist feels and behaves and how the client perceives the therapist. Even though the therapist may not behave with any authority, or use any '*power-over*', clients may still perceive the therapist as doing so. Clients may still not feel they can use their own '*power-from-within*'. However much a PCT therapist refuses to take '*power-over*' the client, there will still be an inequality in terms of how much the therapist and client each feel able to use their '*power-from-within*'. Even though the PCT therapist does not take advantage of this inequality, and in fact provides conditions that aim to reduce it, the therapist still needs to be aware that the client may not perceive the relationship as equally as the therapist does.

Similarly, Burstow (1987) points out that there are areas in which the therapist and client are not necessarily equal or unequal, but where the likelihood is that the therapist will have more power. These areas are in the therapists' level of coping skills and their ability to feel comfortable with life. The inequalities in these areas could be seen as a result of personal histories. She also gives examples of how a client's vulnerability could be missed by a therapist's belief in an equal relationship. However, it is just as likely (if not more so) that clients' coping skills may be much greater than those of the therapist as they may have encountered much more difficult circumstances to cope with. Either way, there is likely to be an inequality of power here arising from personal histories, and this is likely to become apparent in the difference between the client's and therapist's perception of their own '*power-from-within*'. A client's personal history of powerlessness may mean it is difficult for the client to feel their own '*power-from-within*' in the therapy situation, however much a therapist does not use '*power-over*'.

Freeing individuals from normative prescriptions
In PCT the focus is on the facilitative conditions that enable the clients to bring their organismic selves and self-concepts closer together, and thus free them of the oppressive effects of the conditions of worth. This could be seen to address what Foucault describes as the 'stylisation of the self', the ways in which subjects are constituted by power relations and by

discourses around them. Rogers' conditions of worth form a particular theory of how such relations of power constitute an individual. Deconstructive (or narrative) therapists aim to deconstruct relations of power in the lives of clients and to help clients rewrite positive or helpful stories about their lives. The aims of person-centred therapy seem to directly follow the political aims expressed by post-structuralist theorists (see Chapter 4). The implicit (in Foucault), or explicit (in Derrida, or Deleuze and Guattari), political values and aims behind post-structuralist ideas seem to be to free individuals as much as possible from norms that constrain ways of being and feeling. Deleuze and Guattari (1984) emphasise the importance of individuals not repressing their desires to accommodate society. Foucault emphasises the need to expose operations of power and resist the norms that shape and constitute subjects. These values seem to be the same values that lie behind the theory and practice of person-centred therapy. However, PCT aims not just to expose operations of power, but to provide a space for individuals to reconstitute themselves in a way that is beneficial to themselves (i.e. in a way that promotes the actualising tendency). Whereas Foucault refuses to theorise how a positive approach to constituting subjects would work (except by the avoidance of domination), there is some similarity between the values of PCT and those of Deleuze and Guattari (1984). Deleuze and Guattari's notions clearly emphasise the importance of the organismic self (or desire), although for them there would not be one unitary essential self, which is implicit in Rogers' theory.

These very same values also underlie some of Weber's writing on power and his concern about bureaucracy taking away the freedom of the individual (see Chapter 3). Weber was concerned with how an efficient society could operate without constraining individual freedom. However, he was concerned only with the individual freedom of the intellectual elite. Person-centred therapy differs immensely from Weber's elitism in the underlying political beliefs of individual freedom for all.

Structural power in society

In the later part of his life, Rogers began specifically to address concerns about the social context of society and power, and his main contention was that the person-centred approach is a revolutionary way to understand and change oppression, particularly by facilitating communication between the oppressed and the oppressors. Rogers (1978a) argues that the person-centred approach can be used to help people who are members of oppressed groups. He gives an example of a facilitated meeting between 'health consumers', who were poor mainly black people in America, and 'health providers'. He argues that the process of facilitating each person to be heard enabled much greater understanding to be established between both groups. This process meant that all views were heard: there was no necessity for members of the oppressed group to speak with a unified voice in order to be heard. He claims that, as they were heard, members of the oppressed group grew in their confidence to speak and initiate change, and that the group moved to take revolutionary but realistic steps to alter their situation, steps that were later carried out and led to real material change in their conditions.

Rogers comments on the argument that the person-centred approach is a 'soft' approach,

> [a] luxury which may be appropriate for an affluent middle class, but . . . can have no meaning in dealing with an oppressed minority . . . What these groups need are jobs or equal pay or civil rights or educational opportunities — things that must be wrested from the oppressor, that he will not give up willingly. (1978a, p. 105)

He describes Friere's working with Brazilian peasants in 1970 in a way very similar to a person-centred approach, facilitating learning and change within communities. Friere describes the effects of these facilitated group discussions as follows:

> The members, as they reveal themselves to one another, begin to trust themselves as persons, and other members of the group as well. They change their goals. Instead of simply aspiring to become oppressors themselves, they envision a new type of social system, more human. Finally they begin to take considered steps to change the terrible conditions under which they live. (cited in Rogers, 1978a, p. 108)

This explains why Rogers believed his approach to be so revolutionary. Not only does it attempt to improve conditions for people for oppressed groups, but it also works towards changing the whole social system, a system based on hierarchy, power and oppression, to one in which each individual is listened to and considered, and where change is considered from every perspective. Moreover, the means by which Rogers attempts to achieve this are consistent with the goals.

Here the focus on individuals, as opposed to groups of oppressed people, is echoed by Deleuze and Guattari's (1984) focus on the importance for each individual to articulate their own desires and not be constrained by fitting in with group norms (see Chapter 4).

Did Rogers still ignore the material reality of structural positions of power in society?

Waterhouse (1993) compares feminist therapies with person-centred therapy in a feminist critique of person-centred therapy. She points to similarities between the two types of therapy with respect to the importance of equalising counsellor-client relationships and eradicating dualistic thinking. However, she complains that 'In his concept of the person, Rogers consistently neglects to problematise gender, race and class' (p. 58). She contrasts the two approaches, commenting:

> In contrast to Rogers' harmonic view of human relationships, feminists point to the many examples of gender inequality which create profound conflicts of interest between women and men . . . Personal issues, emotional distress and individual breakdown are consequently viewed as political issues . . . Person-centred approaches stress the uniqueness of each person's experience whereas feminist approaches stress the commonality of women's experiences. (Waterhouse, 1993, p. 61)

She claims that, by not recognising the political in the personal, the person-centred therapist is in danger of giving unwarranted weight to individuals' power to effect changes in their everyday lives. She argues that this ignores material or socio-political constraints, and could possibly lead the therapist to collude in blaming the individual for not being able to change. She further seems to imply that a person-centred therapist withholds help or care by the stress on self-reliance, which, as Grant (1990) explains above, is not the case. Despite acknowledging Rogers' awareness of socio-political contexts in his later work, she then discusses his later contributions no further, and thus misses the potential for understanding person-centred therapy in a social context. Both these criticisms seem to be based on misunderstandings of person-centred therapy, which aims to understand an individual's life in its entirety, including the social context. While not assuming that the therapist knows best how to help the client (by, for example, reframing problems in a political context or drawing commonalities with other women's experiences), the therapist would not blame the client, but would simply seek to understand why it is so difficult for the client to change their circumstances.

However, Waterhouse does point out that the emphasis on unique individuals within PCT misses the potential for empowerment by collectivity. The benefits of both these approaches are combined in Rogers' emphasis in his later works on groups in which each individual is listened to as an individual but where the individuals have the opportunity to make their own connections with the experiences of others. This context also minimises the power in the role of the therapist compared with individual therapy.

Waterhouse also makes an important point with respect to the necessity for person-centred therapists to address issues of oppression in training with respect to self-exploration. She explains that 'Without such training the person-centred counsellor is left at best with a vague, and at worst a naïve, view of what it means to be a "person"' (p. 62). She does seem to recognise that there is potential for a person-centred therapist to understand the 'self' to mean 'self-in-social-context', but criticises Rogers for the lack of this emphasis:

> He fails to acknowledge the extent to which our capacity to be empathic is affected by our experience as subjects in a social structure. (p. 66)

Kearney (1996) is much more optimistic about the potential for person-centred therapists to consider the 'self-in-social-context'. She explains the importance of class in therapy, saying:

> Political factors such as class enter into counselling through the power imbalances between client and counsellor, in the language client and counsellor use, in the different class-based meaning structures through which we speak and hear; in the different vocabularies and codes we use and in the different class-based experiences we may have. (p. 77)

She points to the danger of reinforcing the inequality in power in therapy by ignoring class influences. She criticises Waterhouse's (1993) critique of Rogers, suggesting:

> I do not believe that the person-centred focus on the individual necessarily excludes awareness of the social constraints of people's lives in principle, though I believe that it may, and often does, in practice . . . It is, I suggest, perfectly possible to focus on the 'self-actualising tendency of the socially positioned individual' . . . If we hold onto this awareness, I believe it becomes much less likely that we will practise counselling in a way that disregards the oppressive external structures which form the restrictive scaffolding of people's lives. (Kearney, 1996, p. 82)

Kearney further suggests that Rogers himself saw the political radicalness of his approach, and theorised internalised oppression caused by conditions of worth. She contends that person-centred theory is directly concerned with identifying external oppressions. She further emphasises what we need to do to keep the radical sociological and political nature of person-centred therapy:

> I believe that if we regularly fail to challenge our own and our clients' internalised ideologies we lose the radical dimensions of person-centredness and turn it into a much less powerful force for change than it should be. (p. 86)

However, what is important about the way person-centred theory addresses oppression is that each person is understood as an individual: no assumptions or generalisations are made about people from their structural position. This phenomenological position ensures that the individual agency and individuality is acknowledged and that knowledge about social structural conditions should always be in the background of informing understanding about the context of a particular individual's life.

Rogers' theory has been misunderstood to focus exclusively on the concept of the individual, rather than on the individual in relationships and social context. However, PCT already theorises the role of power in the constitution of individuals with respect to the conditions of worth. This incorporates Foucault's ideas of how individuals are constituted in relation to others and by practices of power relations. Thus, PCT is ideally placed to work with socially constituted and positioned individuals.

Conclusion

Is there equality in the person-centred relationship? This depends on which aspects of power in the relationship we are considering. Person-centred therapy certainly challenges the fundamental inequality in the roles of therapist and client in its emphasis on the person-to-person relationship and its focus on the '*power-from-within*' or '*personal power*' of each person. However, this equality is limited by the clients' perception of their own power and thus of that equality, which is also affected by the client's personal history of power and powerlessness.

There is radical potential for PCT to challenge and question the orthodox model of mental illness and to emphasise the autonomy and trustworthiness of the client. In addition, PCT aims to free individuals from normative prescriptions that have constrained individuals, and it has the goal of individual freedom.

The effect of the facilitative conditions is to increase the '*power-from-within*' of the client, and thus the process of therapy aims to equalise any inequalities between the client and therapist from the perspective of how much each can use their '*power-from-within*'. However, there is the danger, in focusing on equality from this perspective, of ignoring other aspects of power. What must also be considered are the material realities of possible inequalities in social structural power, and in the institutional and structural '*power-over*' still attached to the role of therapist, however a therapist may behave.

Chapter 7

The Psychodynamic Approach: isn't the power all in the transference?

This chapter describes the principles of psychodynamic therapy and deconstructs the nature of power in the therapy relationship. The issues are illustrated by my experiences as a client with a psychodynamic therapist.

What is psychodynamic therapy?

Psychodynamic psychotherapy is a form of therapy based on the principles of psychoanalysis. The conditions for psychodynamic therapy are usually less formal than for psychoanalysis. In psychoanalysis, the patient often lies on a couch with the analyst sitting behind the patient's head. In psychodynamic therapy, the *patient* (this is the term usually used by psychodynamic therapists to refer to the person receiving therapy) and therapist may be seated, as in other forms of therapy. Also, in psychoanalysis, appointments are usually frequent, often daily, whereas in psychodynamic therapy appointments tend to be less frequent. Psychodynamic therapy can also be conducted over shorter periods of time than psychoanalysis, which frequently takes place over a period of several years.

The term 'psychodynamic' refers to the way in which the psyche (the mind, the self) is seen as active, not static. Activity is theorised to take place both within the psyche, between different parts of the psyche (intra-psychic), and in relation to others (interpersonal). Different psychoanalytic theorists have mapped the psyche using varying terminology, and different psychoanalytic models place different emphases on varying dynamics. Freud invented psychoanalysis, and after Freud various models of psychoanalysis developed.

The main psychoanalytic models used in clinical practice today include (in the UK): the neo-Freudian model, the object relations school (including the Kleinian model) and the independent school; (in the USA) the ego psychology model, the interpersonal model and, more recently, the self-psychology model and the relational model. Many of these models or schools also have distinct sub-models. Lacan's model of psychoanalysis will not be considered as, despite having profound influences on psychoanalytic theory, his ideas have little influenced the practice of therapy in the UK or USA. However, there are some basic principles shared by all these models which are fundamental to psychodynamic therapy.

Three fundamental principles shared by all psychoanalytic models are described by Spinelli (1994). The first principle he states is the assumption of unconscious mental processes. Freud postulated an area in the psyche, the 'unconscious', which contained material that had no easy access to consciousness. Unconscious material must be inferred, discovered and translated into a conscious form. (This describes the act of interpretation by the therapist.) Freud postulated that some feelings, ideas or even whole experiences are pushed into hiding in the unconscious because they are too threatening or painful for the conscious self to acknowledge. He suggested that these repressed (pushed-into-unconsciousness) feelings were the cause of many symptoms of mental distress, symptoms that resulted from the transformation of these repressed feelings. The aim of psychodynamic therapy is to bring the repressed feelings back into consciousness and to understand them. Malan (1979) suggests that people adopt various defences to avoid pain and conflict. He represents this by the concept of his 'triangle of conflict'. This triangle, with the apex at the base, has anxiety (about the threatening feeling) at one of the top points, defence at the other, and the hidden feeling at the base (see Fig. 7a). One aim of psychodynamic therapy is to link the different points of the triangle, and to use the presented anxiety and defence to interpret the hidden feeling in the unconscious.

The second principle suggested by Spinelli (1994) is that the past is the cause of current behaviour. Jacobs (1988) explains that 'All psycho-dynamic theories pay attention to the importance of a child's early environment as promoting the foundation of later personality strength or weakness' (p. 6). He stresses that what is important is not just how the child is treated, but also how the child fantasises about the world. He suggests that these early relationships (between the child and parental figures) influence later relationships with the adult, repeating early relationship dynamics, but often in a distorted way. One of the aims of the psychodynamic therapist is to establish links between patterns in early and current relationships.

The third fundamental principle suggested by Spinelli (1994) is that of transference and countertransference. This phenomenon was first hypothesised by Freud, who suggested that the patients' feelings about and reactions to early relationships were repeated in their relationship with the therapist. Countertransference originally referred to the therapist's unconscious feelings from the past being repeated with the patient, but it is generally used now to refer to any feelings the therapist has about the patient. Another aim of the psychodynamic therapist is to interpret this transference, that is to make links between the therapy relationship and current or past relationships in the patient's life. Malan (1979) describes this as the triangle of the person. Again, the apex of the triangle is at the base; the two top points represent other (O) (usually current relationships) and transference (T) (the relationship with the therapist). Relationships with parents (P) is at the base apex of the triangle (see Fig. 7b). He describes the aim as to use the top two apexes of the triangle to interpret, and thus connect with, the base apex of the patient's early relationships.

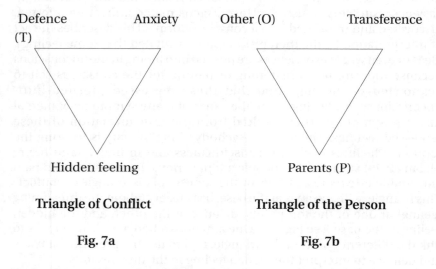

Defence   Anxiety   Other (O)   Transference
(T)

Hidden feeling   Parents (P)

Triangle of Conflict   **Triangle of the Person**

Fig. 7a   **Fig. 7b**

In the process of psychoanalysis, the patient is expected to 'free-associate', i.e. say everything that comes into their mind. This process is not emphasised as much in psychodynamic therapy. However, in both psychoanalysis and psychodynamic therapy, the therapist aims to bring the patient's unconscious feelings to the surface for the patient to experience them consciously. Malan explains:

> For this purpose the therapist uses theoretical knowledge, guided wherever possible by his own self-knowledge, to identify himself with the patient; and puts his understanding to the patient in the form of interpretations which constitute his main therapeutic tool. (1979, p. 74)

As well as achieving change through insight (the patient's understanding of their repressed emotions and the dynamics of their psyche), there is an additional aim of providing in the therapy relationship a 'corrective emotional experience' to the conflict in the transference (Malan, 1979, p. 140). However, therapists in psychodynamic therapy are also governed by the 'rule of abstinence', which suggests that they should not bring their subjectivity to the therapy relationship, but should provide themselves merely as an object for the patient to use and transfer to as necessary. Both Jacobs (1988) and Malan (1979) suggest, however, that there are times when it is appropriate for the therapist to provide more than interpretation. Malan (1979) clarifies this balance, saying that 'the aim of therapy is not to make up to patients for the love that they have missed, but to help them work through their feelings about not having it' (p. 141). But he also suggests that there are times when it is appropriate to give 'a parent's care in ways that are essentially symbolic, do not step beyond the bounds of the therapeutic situation, and yet are something more than just making interpretations' (p. 142). This balance between interpretation and responding to the patient emotionally within the therapy relationship provokes much debate and disagreement within the literature on psychodynamic therapy. I am arguing that where this balance lies with particular therapists and theories has important implications with respect to power in the therapy relationship.

Psychoanalytic theorising of power in relation to structural power

In this section I present some theories of power that use psychoanalysis, and also some critiques of psychoanalysis (mainly feminist) with respect to power. Some authors (such as Maguire, 1995; Sayers, 1986; Hurvitz, 1973; Sampson, 1965; Benjamin, 1988 and Butler, 1990) criticise psychoanalytic theory for failing to challenge the subordination of women. Most of these authors also suggest how psychoanalytic theory can be used to challenge structural relations of power and domination.

Structures and agency: feminism and psychoanalysis

Maguire (1995) categorises the effects of the 'male bias' in psychoanalytic theories, contending that psychoanalytic theory continues the subordination of women. She suggests that psychoanalytic theory could be useful in understanding the difficulties for women of asserting their right to equality in relationships. This could be done by taking into account the way that social factors 'including real sex discrimination and devaluation, interact with psychic difficulties in separating from the mother' (p. 120). She continues:

> Experiences of powerlessness and exclusion are inevitable in childhood. But it is not inevitable that they should become subsumed into a distorted view of sexual difference as children become aware of their position in the gender hierarchy. (p. 120)

She also suggests that gender is an important factor to consider in therapy:

> Psychotherapy is no more immune to issues of gender-based power
> and status than any other arena of activity — indeed the very nature
> of the therapeutic enterprise makes it inevitable that such issues
> will be at the heart of the therapist-client relationship. (p. 133)

Here Maguire is considering both structures of power, and their interaction with and mutually constitutive (co-creating) effects on individual agency. She seems to be synthesising structural feminist concepts of power and post-structural concepts of interrelationships and the constitutive effects of power (see Chapters 3 and 4). However, the focus is still on subjects (or individuals), and not on relationships and networks of power. She suggests that psychoanalysis can be used to try to understand the interactions between individuals and structures with respect to power, and that this understanding could challenge men's domination.

Sayers (1986) explores the contributions of psychoanalytic theorists to the analysis of gender relations. She considers *essentialist*[1] theorists such as Irigaray and argues that femininity is defined in patriarchy not on its own, but in relation to masculinity, and that the essence of femininity is used to justify rather than question social inequalities. She claims that we need to go beyond essentialist stereotypes of sexual difference and to challenge these stereotypes. We cannot accept the location of differences in biology.

Sayers considers Klein, object relations theorists and Lacan and their accounts of women's acceptance of subordination. However, Sayers claims that they fail to account for women's resistance. She summarises by saying that different theorists attend either to women's differences from men (for example Horney, Lacan), to the neglect of their similarities, or to similarities (for example Dinnerstein), to the neglect of their differences. She contends that Freud is virtually alone in considering how men and women's psychology is determined by their similarities and differences in their social and biological lot, although she suggests that, with Freud's focus on the psychic reality of his patients, he often overlooked the contradictions in their material reality. Sayers (1986) contends that psychoanalysis aims to bring conflicts and frustration to consciousness. She suggests that conscious awareness of conflicts in women's social lot is an essential precondition for feminist action in women and that collective feminist struggle is necessary to achieve liberation. For feminism, she suggests, psychoanalysis is only the beginning.

Like Maguire (1995), Sayers puts together structural feminist concepts of power with a concept of individual agency and a mutually constitutive relationship between the two. Similarly, she suggests a role for psychoanalysis as a way to raise awareness of power in relationships as a precursor to political collective action.

---

1. Essentialism argues that men and women are inherently, innately, biologically or psychologically different. Essentialist feminists argue that women should use their differences to challenge patriarchy and present a new way of being.

Psychoanalysis and women's oppression

Hurvitz (1973) described how psychoanalytic theories have continued the subordination of women by supporting the established order of society. He described how these theories have fostered a view of women as 'appendages to men', encouraging conditions and attitudes that create problems for many women. Then, women are encouraged to accept this view in psychotherapy. Here, Hurvitz seems to have simplistically analysed psychodynamic psychology, as though this were one theory. As Sayers (1986) demonstrates, there are many psychoanalytic theorists who do not present the essentialist perspective that he describes. He thus fails to acknowledge the potential of other theories to point to the interaction of psychic and social phenomena, and to suggest ways forward to challenge domination and structures of power.

Freud's theorising on the origins of power and dominance: lack of social analysis

Sampson (1965) theorised the psychology of power from a psychoanalytic perspective. He described Freud's theory of power, dominance and submission in relationships. Freud suggested that the *Oedipus conflict*[2] is resolved by the child deferring to paternal authority, and Sampson therefore suggests that Freud's theory is that infantile love is based on authority. According to Sampson, Freud suggests that there is a necessity for government in society because of people's unconscious longings for paternal despotism.

Freud also proposes that there is an innate drive in people towards aggression and power. According to Freud, the unequal characteristics of people lead to the aggressive power instinct, the will to subjugate another for one's own purposes, and he suggests that this drive lies at the root of every relationship. This instinct is also hypothesised by Nietzsche, who termed it the 'will to power' and claimed it to be the most powerful innate drive in all humans (see Chapter 4). Humans enter into dominance and submission relations, and Sampson suggests that fear of insecurity leads to the wish to take power. He contends that the price of this is that dominance is inseparable from arrogance and submission inseparable from resentment, and that these emotions get in the way of love in relationships. For Freud, the aim in psychoanalysis was for patients to become aware of this will to power and to control it. However, Sampson's contention is that Freud's analysis of power relations is insufficient, as he failed to challenge the inequality of the sexes and so underestimated people's psychic ability to overcome aggression and the need for authority.

Deleuze and Guattari (1984), in *Anti-Oedipus: Capitalism and*

---

2. The Oedipus conflict was a key stage in the development of a child for Freud. He hypothesised that the male child, who loves his mother, realises he is in competition for his mother's love with the father. He resolves the conflict by deferring to paternal authority.

Schizophrenia, provide a critique of the basis of psychoanalytic theory, the Oedipus complex. They contend that the Oedipus myth prohibits incest, thus implicitly suggesting that people desire incest. However, they claim that this provides a displacement of what is threatening to society, which is desire itself — each individual's own wants and feelings — which may conflict with the stability of society. The Oedipus myth gives a justification for psychic repression of individuals. Thus, psychoanalysis is used as an instrument of repression. The authors suggest that this psychic repression is necessary for social repression. They hypothesise that social repression is dependent on desire through sexual repression and the family as the agent of psychic repression. They suggest that, by substituting incest for desire, the interest for social production is evident, 'for the latter could not otherwise ward off desire's potential for revolt and revolution' (p. 120).

Benjamin (1988) provides a critique of Freud's theory of dominance and power in relationships. She agrees with Sampson's (1965) contention, explaining:

> What is extraordinary about the discussion of authority throughout Freudian thought is that it occurs exclusively in a world of men . . . woman's subordination to man is taken for granted, invisible . . . This assumption . . . provides . . . the ultimate rationalisation for accepting all authority. (p. 6)

Benjamin contends that psychoanalytic theory provides the basis for the continuation of dualistic thought and relations, by the genesis of the psychic structure in which one person plays the subject and the other must serve as his object. This forms the fundamental premise of domination. She suggests instead that

> Domination and submission result from a breakdown of the necessary tension between self-assertion and mutual recognition[3] that allows self and other to meet as sovereign equals. (1988, p. 12)

Benjamin asserts that many psychoanalytic theories have missed the need for mutual recognition in their emphasis on the mother as the object of the child's needs: the child needs to see its mother as an independent subject, not just as an object. Psychoanalytic theories have emphasised the need for autonomy at the expense of mutuality. She suggests that the basic pattern of domination is set in motion by the denial of recognition to the original 'other', the mother, and that the resulting structure of subject and object is represented by male and female. Rather than being inevitable, she suggests that

---

3. Benjamin (1988) hypothesises that there are two conflicting drives within each person: first, the drive to independence and autonomy, which is emphasised by object relations theorists; second, the need for recognition, for one's individuality to be recognised by another individual who is also a subject in their own right, rather than an object of one's needs.

> Domination . . . is the twisting of the bonds of love. Domination does
> not repress the desire for recognition; rather, it enlists and transforms
> it . . . For the person who takes this route to establishing his own
> power, there is an absence where the other should be. (p. 217)

Benjamin contends that to halt this cycle of domination and submission, the other (the first other being the mother) must make a difference: women must claim their subjectivities. Whereas power is inevitable as the interplay and tension of the needs for recognition and independence, 'If the denial of recognition does not become frozen into unmoveable relationships, the play of power need not be hardened into domination' (1988, p. 223). Here, Benjamin concentrates on the agency of individuals and their ability to change structures of power. There could be a danger here of concentrating just on an individual's abilities to overcome structures of power without acknowledging the pervasiveness and longevity of these structures. There may also be the danger of challenging women to change things here, with the result that women could be blamed if they are unable to change their relations of power. This focus on one part of the complex web of power relations leaves unnoticed the other parts in these relations.

Frosh (1997) criticises psychoanalysis for its 'ethnocentricity', but, like Sayers (1986), suggests that psychoanalysis can be an adjunct to social analyses. He argues that

> Rationality does not sufficiently explain what goes on as people
> struggle for generations to make real some kind of dream; something
> else is at work, irreducible to economic or political cause. (p. 239)

Again, the model used is of the importance of both structures and agency, each irreducible to the other.

Fanon (1986) provides a psychoanalytic theory of how oppression works on the unconscious. He analyses relationships between black and white people in conditions of colonialism and investigates how racism affects both on an unconscious level. In analysing the effects of racism on black people, Fanon notes that the black person is living his life for The Other (the white person), 'because it is The Other who corroborates him in his search for self-validation' (p. 213). He suggests that self-consciousness and desire as steps to recognition can obtain freedom and life. He argues against essentialism and insists that each black person must be treated as an individual. He criticises the notion of history and a collective unconscious as preventing change:

> The body of history does not determine a single one of my actions.
> I am my own foundation. And it is by going beyond the historical,
> instrumental foundation hypothesis that I will initiate the cycle of
> my freedom . . . The Negro is not. Any more than the white man.
> (Fanon, 1986, p. 231)

Both Fanon (1986) and Benjamin (1988) suggest that the solution is mutual recognition, which has the potential to set a different template for relationships, from one of domination and oppression to one of mutual respect. Fanon explains: 'Superiority? Inferiority? Why not the simple attempt to touch the other, to feel the other, to explain the other to myself?' (p. 231).

Fanon again provides an analysis of structures of power that acknowledges the position of individual subjects and their internal life as a relevant part in the net of power relations. He abstains from essentialism, but has a tendency to suggest, along with Butler (1990), that individuals can change relations of power alone. Both Fanon and Butler miss the potential of Arendt's concept of power and Starhawk's (1987) concept of '*power-with*', of the possibility of the positive power of collectivity (see Chapter 3). They tend to isolate the individual as a unit of analysis and to suggest the individual as a locus for change, which can miss the positive interactive relationships between the individual and others.

Butler (1990) criticises psychoanalytic theory, accusing it of gender essentialism. She argues that psychoanalytic theories institute gender coherence through the stabilising meta-narrative of infantile development, which 'instantiates gender specificity and subsequently informs, organises and unifies identity' (p. 329). She notes that psychoanalytic theory excludes discontinuities and claims a fixed categorical polarity between maleness and femaleness, both biologically and psychologically, which does not exist. She suggests that psychoanalysis as an account of gender development fails to account for itself as a narrative, and submits from Nietzsche and Foucault that psychoanalytic theory inscripts laws on the body and constitutes the subject (see Chapter 4). She contends that Foucault suggests that the notion of gender being fixed internally, and only then being manifest externally, creates

> the illusion of an interior and organising gender core, an illusion discursively maintained for the purpose of the regulation of sexuality within the obligatory frame of reproductive heterosexuality. (pp. 336–7)

Butler notes that to locate the cause of desire in the 'self' precludes an analysis of the political constitution of the gendered subject. She calls for resistance to this concept, saying:

> it seems crucial to resist the myth of interior origins, understood either as naturalised or culturally fixed. Only then, gender coherence might be understood as the regulatory fiction that it is — rather than the common point of our liberation. (p. 339)

Here, Butler uses post-structural ideas from Foucault to perform an analysis of the effects of psychoanalytic theory on the constitution of subjects. She criticises the notion of the essential gendered subject and emphasises the importance of resisting psychoanalytic claims to a psychological coherent and fixed gendered subject. Similarly, Frosh (1997, p. 231) criticises psychoanalysis for its 'normative moralising'.

The therapy relationship in psychodynamic therapy

Jacobs (1988) suggests that there are three aspects to the therapy relationship: the transference relationship, the 'equal relationship' and the 'working relationship'. The *transference relationship* refers to the way the patient interacts with the therapist as a result of the history of their relationship, repeating relationship dynamics from previous important relationships. The therapist's role is to interpret the transference, i.e. to make connections between dynamics in the therapy relationship and dynamics in other relationships, including parental relationships, for the patient. Jacobs suggests that the *equal relationship* refers to the fact that the therapist and the patient share a common humanity which unites them. This aspect of the relationship refers to the therapist's caring response to the patient. He describes the *working relationship* as the agreement between the therapist and patient to co-operate in trying to understand certain less adult and less mature aspects of the patient. He suggests that this concept describes two people working together on a problem. He also notes that transference can interfere with this. In the following sections I discuss each of these aspects of the therapy relationship with reference to power.

The therapist's power in the transference relationship

Power in the transference relationship was a strong feature in my experience of the therapy relationship as a client with a psychodynamic therapist. When my therapist made interpretations about what she believed to be happening in the therapy relationship, I felt relatively powerless to disagree. At times I did disagree, and sometimes this was respected. When this occurred the interpretations, being tentative and respectful, had a very different feel to me, and were much more likely to be helpful even if they did not make complete sense. However, at other times I felt that the therapist was continuing to make the same interpretation, challenging my different understanding of the situation. Indeed, often my 'resistance' to her interpretations was interpreted as evidence of the transference. At these times I started to doubt my ability to know what I was feeling, and I subscribed to the view of the therapist as 'expert', whom I expected to know better than I. This is unsurprising, given how the psychoanalytic discourse of transference positions the patient as unaware of their unconscious, with defences to be broken and insights to be provided by the expert therapist. I was positioned very much within this discourse as the patient without knowledge (PwK: Madigan, 1999), and the effect was that I began to doubt my own knowledge of myself.

Spinelli (1994) criticises the concept of transference, and the therapist's position to interpret transference as a position of unquestionable power. He explains that transference is generally understood to be related to the patient's inappropriate emotional responses to the therapist, but it is not clear how the therapist is to distinguish between appropriate and inappropriate responses. He quotes Shlien (1984), who suggests that transference points to the imbalance of power in the therapy relationship: 'For, through its use, the therapist alone becomes the person in the relationship who is able to declare which emotional responses are appropriate and which are inappropriate' (p. 185). Spinelli further contends that

> analytic interpretations place therapists in a position of great power
> since they rely on their abilities to understand and reveal the hidden
> meanings in their clients' statements and behaviours, before they are
> consciously acknowledged by the clients themselves. (1994, p. 199)

He concludes that this power gives therapists the ability to know the 'truth', which must be accepted by the clients in order for them to 'get better'.

Frosh (1997) comments on the firm place for authority in psychoanalytic theory and therapy. He suggests that 'psychoanalysis is built heavily around the structures of authority' (p. 6). He further notes the place of authority in the training of psychoanalysts, saying: 'Introduction into the analytic world, it seems, is not a matter of learning certain skills, but of absorbing certain values, more than that, it is a matter of bowing the head to authority' (p. 7). He summarises the case against psychoanalysis as follows:

> Psychoanalysis is criticised for its procedures, which in the most
> extreme characterisation are seen as domineering, constricting,
> expensive, elitist, speculative, intrusive, patriarchal and socially
> oppressive. (p. 236)

The power of the psychodynamic therapist's position to define reality is further confirmed by Clinchy (1996, p. 214). She quotes Schwaber (1983, pp. 386, 390) who similarly suggests that 'analytic listening remains steeped in a hierarchical two-reality view . . . the one the patient experiences, and the one the analyst "knows"'. Clinchy instead suggests that the two realities are relative rather than hierarchical. Maguire (1995) further elucidates this position: 'This exclusive reliance on interpreting the transference gives the analyst enormous power to define what is happening in the therapeutic relationship' (p. 170). Aron (1996) explains that Klein was worried about extending the concept of countertransference from repeated feelings from the analyst's past to all the analyst's feelings.

She was 'worried that such a usage of these concepts would lead analysts to blame patients for their own difficulties' (p. 209). Thus, the concepts of transference and countertransference can be used to enable the therapist to blame the patient for whatever feelings there are in the relationship.

Frosh (1997) also notes the power of transference and observes how this limits any criticism of psychoanalysis from within it, as any feelings can be interpreted as transference. He points out the confusion of reality by the power of transference:

> The power of this account is very great in numerous ways . . . it makes it very difficult to know when to stop; that is, it makes reality so completely imbued with fantasy that one can never be confident about calibrating anything — any excess or persecution, any act of love or generosity. Motives become obscured, not clarified; interpretation can be a weapon. (p. 12)

He notes that the claim of a dynamic unconscious also serves the function of exploding all claims to absolute knowledge; there is never an objective place to stand. Yet, the therapist is seen to be in a position to define what is happening. The psychodynamic therapist has the authority to 'know' the unconscious and interpret transference. Frosh considers this 'knowledge' and notes that different psychoanalytic theorists have had various attitudes towards the therapist's knowledge. Lacan suggested no one could know. Similarly, Bion encouraged analysts to enter work without memory or desire. For Bion, the analyst's authority lay in their open attitude to finding out. However, Frosh also notes that this is not the general stance of psychoanalytic theory, which makes many claims to truth although some schools of psychoanalysis are aware of the importance of not knowing 'truth', such as the independent school.

Masson (1989) suggests that Ferenczi first realised the aggressiveness or power behind the therapist's interpretation. He suggests that

> This may be the first occasion when an analyst recognised (or at least acknowledged) that an interpretation can be an act of aggression. Ferenczi had intruded, in an invasive manner, on the thought process of another person. And he knew it . . . In a sense every interpretation is an invasion, an intrusion, and a confrontation. (Masson, 1989, p. 117)

Masson also mentions Ferenczi's recognition of the power of the therapist with regard to the transference feelings, and the difficulty for the patient to leave therapy, because of the transference relationship.

Many times during my therapy I felt that I wanted to discontinue the therapy. Most times this wish was interpreted with respect to the transference relationship, the implication being that if I left I would be running away from an 'issue', and I should stay and work through it. The idea of my wanting to leave being avoidance may have been true at times, or to some extent. However, the biggest problem I found with this interpretation of the transference was that, if I accepted it, then the total responsibility for the dynamic felt always to be placed with me. My therapist did not seem to accept any position for her role in the relationship or her role in 'provoking' a particular transference reaction. There were other times when I was angry about her behaviour, for example when she appeared (to me) to be cold and uncaring. Again, this was interpreted with respect to my history, the implication being that the current (therapy) relationship was not relevant beyond being a tool to point out the past; and my therapist's behaviour, which may have also influenced my perception of her as cold and uncaring, was never on the agenda.

Ferenczi suggested that the therapist's authoritarian stance and 'rule of abstinence' encouraged certain transference reactions based on the power differential and encouraged patients to relate to therapists as parental figures. Masson explains:

> Ferenczi said that the analyst infantilises patients. Far from helping them to overcome infantile problems, the analyst resubmerges them in a relationship in which it is the analyst who emerges as all-powerful. (1989, p. 122)

Masson also notes that Ferenczi recognised that the imbalance of power that was underlying the abuse of children also existed in the therapy relationship. Obviously, the way my therapist behaved towards me influenced my feelings towards her, 'transference' or not; there must have been many transference responses from my history that she could have provoked. However, by interpreting my feelings with respect to transference, only the relevance of *my* history was open for discussion, and the relevance of *her* behaviour was never acknowledged.

Midway through my therapy, I moved to the city where my therapist lived and worked, a move that I had considered before starting my therapy. She interpreted this move as my desire to be closer to her. I disagreed with this interpretation, but she persisted in making the same interpretation over the weeks. This issue was complex. There certainly was truth in my wish to be closer to her, which I felt was about her coldness in the way she related to me, although I did not think this feeling was relevant to my moving. But her persistence with this interpretation only resulted in my doubting my own feelings, resenting her persistence and in becoming less able to discuss my feelings about her. It certainly did not enable learning to take place. If she had been more tentative with her interpretation and had listened to my reasons for disagreeing, I am sure that would have enabled me to discuss the aspects of truth in her suggestions; but her persistence had the effect of my becoming more determined to find no truth in her interpretations.

Szasz (1963) describes the origins of, and criticises the notion of, transference. From Freud, the concept of transference has been used to describe the patient's love for the analyst; this was later extended to include other strong feelings for the analyst. Szasz notes that according to the patient this experience is real, whereas according to Freud it is an illusion (transference). He suggests:

> In these cases there is a conflict of opinion between the patient and physician, which is not resolved by examination of the merits of the two views, but rather by the physician's autocratic judgement: his view is correct, and is considered 'reality'; the patient's view is incorrect and is considered 'transference'. (Szasz, 1963, p. 432)

He continues: 'Workmanlike use of the concept of transference should not blind us to the fact that the term is not a neutral description but rather the analyst's judgement of the patient's behaviour' (p. 433). He distinguishes between transference as the analyst's judgement and as the patient's experience. He points out that, when both agree that it is transference, learning can take place. However, if the analyst considers the patient's behaviour to be transference and the patient does not, then, 'Regardless of who is correct, analyst or patient, such disagreement precludes analysis of the transference' (p. 434).

The therapy situation did elicit strong feelings in me about my therapist, but it felt as if there were a huge imbalance in the situation; that only my feelings were on the agenda, and only my part in the relationship. By the constant focus on my history, my therapist took no responsibility for her part in our relationship. Szasz (1963) suggests that transference serves as a defence for the analyst. He claims that the concept provides a safety barrier to prevent the therapist acting out on their feelings:

> The analytic situation is thus a paradox: it stimulates, and at the same time frustrates, the development of an intense human relationship. In a sense, analyst and patient tease each other. The analytic situation requires that each participant have strong experiences, and yet not act on them. (p. 437)

Szasz suggests that the concept of transference protects the analyst by allowing them to believe that the patient's strong emotions are directed not at them, but towards internal objects. He clarifies the effect of this:

> The patient does not really love or hate the analyst, but someone else. What could be more reassuring? This is why so-called transference interpretations are so easily and so often misused: they provide a ready-made opportunity for putting the patient at arm's length. (p. 348)

Szasz justifies this idea with reference to the origins of transference. Freud created the concept of transference with reference to Breuer's analysis of Anna O. At the time Breuer was overwhelmed by Anna O's feelings towards him, and Freud's concept of transference reassured him that Anna O's erotic feelings were not actually towards him. Szasz explains:

> Breuer, it appears, was overcome by the 'reality' of his relationship with Anna O. The threat of the patient's eroticism was effectively tamed by Freud when he created the concept of transference: the analyst could henceforth tell himself that he was not the genuine object, but a mere symbol of his patient's desire. (p. 443)

Szasz suggests that 'The notion of transference is reassuring to therapists precisely because it implies a denial (or mitigation) of the "personal" in the analytic situation' (p. 442). He pointed out that this was perhaps necessary for Freud in the historical context of the nineteenth century, noting that,

> in psychoanalysis, what stands between obscenity and science is the concept of transference. This concept and all it implies, renders the physician a non-participant in the latter's preoccupation with primary emotions. (p. 442)

I certainly felt that, by constantly interpreting the transference and focusing the attention on the origin of my feelings from past relationships, my therapist could remove her 'person' from the relationship, and her responsibility for her way of relating which provoked my feelings. It felt to me that she was never there as a person in her own right, but merely as a 'therapist', a 'blank screen' for my projections. I experienced this as very cold, uncaring and withholding. I also felt that my total responsibility for the therapy relationship, which I felt she gave me by constant transference interpretations, was an unhelpful responsibility to shoulder.

The idea that a therapist can be purely a container or object for the client's transference projections is analogous to positioning the therapist as an objective observer, as opposed to a person in the relationship. This possibility in any kind of human relationship or interaction has been critiqued from feminist and social constructionist perspectives. The possibility of a therapist remaining neutral and objective in such an intimate connection as a therapy relationship is even more open to these criticisms.

I constantly doubted my feelings about my therapist and how she was behaving in the therapy relationship with me, as these feelings were inevitably interpreted as transference. It was impossible to have a discussion about her behaviour, without this being reduced to my transference reactions. Szasz points out the danger of the concept of transference. In introducing the concept of the therapist as a symbol, the therapist is rendered invulnerable as a person. He explains: 'When an object becomes a symbol (of another object), people no longer react to it as an object; hence, its features qua object become inscrutable' (p. 442). Thus, the danger is 'because it tends to place the person of the analyst beyond the reality testing of patients, colleagues, and self' (p. 443). Further,

> The use of the concept of transference in psychotherapy thus led to two different results. On the one hand, it enabled the analyst to work where we could not otherwise have worked: on the other, it exposed him to the danger of being 'wrong' vis-à-vis his patient — and of abusing the analytic relationship — without anyone being able to demonstrate this to him. (p. 442)

This point is echoed by Frosh (1997), when he points out the difficulties of criticising psychoanalysis from within. Szasz concludes that to be an ethical therapist requires much integrity; but this can only be taken on trust:

> No-one, psychoanalysts included, has as yet discovered a method to make people behave with integrity when no-one is watching. Yet this is the kind of integrity analytic work requires of the analyst. (Szasz, 1963, p. 442)

The discourse of transference had the effect of completely trapping me as someone unable to trust her own knowledge; my disagreeing with interpretations was used as further evidence of my defences and as even more reason not to trust me. The fact that there was some sense in some of the interpretations, at least in part, made it even harder for me to trust my own knowledge and feelings. This effect was hardly surprising, given the nature of the psychoanalytic discourse about the therapist as 'expert', and the patient being rife with immature unconscious defences.

The working alliance

Sterba (1981) first described the ego split, which was used for the concept of the working or treatment alliance. He hypothesised that part of the patient's ego becomes part of the analysis of their experiencing self, and the therapist allies themselves with this part of the ego against the forces of instinct and repression. Taking this concept further, Greenson (1981a) added the concept of the 'real' relationship, i.e. the patient's realistic view of the therapist as a person. Grostein suggests that these concepts grew from the realisation that, in addition to the importance of transference, there is another parallel track of realistic understanding between two human beings. This seems to be more related to Jacobs' concept of the 'equal relationship'. The 'real' relationship and the 'working alliance' seem to be distinct but overlapping concepts, both containing aspects that do not fit with the other; i.e. part of the working alliance may stem from the positive transference relationship, and part of the real relationship may not consist of positive feelings towards the therapy.

Sandler et al. (1992) consider the working alliance as a broad concept, 'a composite of all those factors that keep the patient in treatment and enable him to remain there during phases of resistance and hostile transference' (p. 34). They suggest that there is increasing recognition of the need for 'a basically friendly or "human" quality in the analyst'. However, they also suggest that the alliance has no value in and of itself. They emphasise the use of the therapeutic alliance as a means to analyse resistances and transference. They also stress the danger in using the concept to avoid transference. Thus, this concept seems to be one that maximises the power of the therapist to keep the patient in therapy, and perhaps engages on an intellectual rather than emotional level with the patient. It seems to be the concept of the therapeutic alliance that acknowledges the importance of consent and autonomy for the patient.

My experience in therapy was that my therapist constantly seemed to ally herself with the part of me that wanted to stay in therapy (for positive and negative, realistic and false reasons). I felt that the parts of me that considered ending and the parts of me that were angry and disillusioned with her behaviour were considered to be 'immature' and definitely not to be acted upon. This felt like yet another way of invalidating my negative feelings in relation to her and her behaviour. It felt as if my therapist believed she was validating the part of me wanting to stay in therapy at the expense of the part of me that was not happy with what was happening — 'in my best interests'. The danger in this seems to be the assumption that she is a rational unified being, and thus would be free from believing that her actions were 'in my best interests' while at the same time they were actually serving a purpose for her. Her alliance with the part of me that wanted to stay in therapy, for example, could have worked in her interest, enabling her to defend herself against my negative feelings towards her, or even serving a financial purpose for her by keeping me paying for therapy. Each time I felt angry or unhappy about her way of relating to me, I am sure she could justify it as being 'in my best interests' to interpret my transference reaction; at the same time, this enabled her to avoid taking responsibility for her part in the relationship.

Maroda (1994) criticises the notion of the therapeutic alliance. She asks:

> How can we communicate to the patient that we trust him and want
> to work with him, yet at the next moment take the attitude that he
> is trying to lead us down the proverbial road to hell? (p. 23)

She suggests that this is what happens if the therapist tries to ally themselves with part of the patient and regard the other part as the enemy. Further,

> It seems to me that the most that can be achieved this way is a
> relationship consisting of alternating alliances and misalliances,
> which can only last or succeed to the degree that both patient and

therapist perceive each other to be well-intentioned. The perception of the patient as a person who attempts to derail the therapist, is, I believe, the single most faulty aspect of the psychodynamic approach. (Maroda, 1994, p. 23)

Hinshelwood (1997) problematises the whole notion of informed consent in psychoanalysis. He claims that psychoanalytic theory postulates a divided psyche — divided between conscious and unconscious, and also within the conscious, according to object relations theorists. He suggests that the interpersonal Kleinian concepts of *splitting, projection* and *introjection*[4] seriously hamper the idea of a unitary subject who is capable of giving informed consent. He also suggests that there is some debate over the possibility of there being an area of the mind (hypothesised to form the alliance) that is free from transference. He suggests that, instead of the principle of an alliance which consents, therapists should work from the ethical principle of integration. An intervention that promotes the patient's integration, and consequently their ability to self-reflect and make decisions, is ethically justified.

The psychoanalytic divided subject has implications for relations of power. The non-unitary, non-rational subject theorised by psychoanalysis suggests that power is always inherent in relationships, and that conflict is also intra-psychic. This divided and dynamic subject theorised by psychoanalysis causes difficulties with issues of control, decision-making and consent. Different parts of the subject may make different decisions, and these decisions may change over time. Thus, if a psychodynamic therapist is making judgements for the patient, this is another area where there are ethical implications, and supervision is essential to check that the reasons for decisions are justified and legitimately in the interests of the client. Ethical principles such as integration, as suggested by Hinshelwood (1997), will be essential to lead and judge the therapist's decisions.

However, a principle like this also enables the therapist to justify making decisions 'in the best interests of the client' — which may in fact not be the case. The whole concept of consent not being possible with a non-unified subject puts the idea of autonomy on very dangerous grounds, and completely removes the person of the psychoanalytic therapist from criticism. An alternative to Hinshelwood's principle of integration could be the acceptance of all parts of the non-unified self equally, which would leave much more responsibility and autonomy in the hands of the client. If my therapist had listened and respected equally all the different sides of me that wanted and did not want to stay in therapy, I would have been

---

4. Klein described these 'primitive' phenomena in psychoanalysis. She described 'splitting' in patients where there seemed to be something missing in their relating to others, a blankness of affect. She also described 'projective identification', which supports the splitting process, by projecting the split part of the mind into another person. Similarly, 'introjection' is the process by which someone receives a split and projected part of another's mind. She hypothesised that these phenomena occur in therapy between the patient and therapist and in everyday life relations.

enabled to make my own decision about whether to continue at each point. However, with this principle, consent would be ongoing and would be made on the basis of the client's experiences and knowledge available, and would need to be repeatedly checked out.

I believe that I finally managed to leave therapy only because, after four and a half years, my therapist did not seem to object to the idea or to continue to interpret my desire to leave as my running away from something. It felt that carrying out my decision to leave was based on whether she agreed with the 'rationality' of my decision. In retrospect, this concerns me very much when I realise how my autonomy, consent and responsibility for my own decisions were compromised to such an extent.

The 'equal' or 'real' relationship

Grostein (1990) noted the balance from the beginnings of psychoanalysis between interpreting the transference and an empathic or 'real' relationship between the therapist and patient — the balance between rigour in analysis and humanism. He pointed out that Freud himself was not above organising food and money for his patients. He also points to Ferenczi as being particularly interested in empathy and recommending changing the atmosphere of analysis from one of austerity and authority to an emotional climate for empathic functioning. Masson (1989) describes Ferenczi's emphasis on the emotional side of the therapy relationship. He suggested that Ferenczi believed that the therapist should give up authority for successful analysis. Following this idea, Ferenczi experimented with mutual analysis. Masson suggests that 'Analysis has never had anything comforting about it' (p. 129).

Freud, when he first heard from his patients tales of their sexuality and sexual relationships with adults as infants, believed that his patients had been sexually abused. But later he abandoned this 'seduction theory', in favour of one suggesting that his infants had fantasised about sexual relationships with their parents, and in therapy remembered their fantasies rather than actual abuse. Commenting on Ferenczi's observations of Freud's abandonment of the seduction theory and its replacement by the universal fantasies of children, Masson explains:

> Therapy, Freud maintained, does not require any deep emotional commitment, but merely a certain intellectual grasp of theory. In effect, said Ferenczi, Freud's heart was no longer in therapy, because he could no longer believe in the uniqueness of the reality of each separate human being's experience of suffering, thereby robbing it of its power to move us individually. (p. 131)

Masson suggests that the result of this backward step by Freud is to leave the therapist in the position of making moral judgements.

It felt to me that most feelings I had about therapy, or about my therapist, were a mixture of real and transference components. Often interpreting the transference was useful, but I believe that acknowledging the real components would also have been useful. I am not contesting that some of my reactions and feelings were relevant to past relationships, but they were also relevant to the therapy relationship I was in, and this felt to me to be never considered. It seemed that my therapist took no responsibility for her part in our relationship, her only relevance being to point to my past issues, and this left me feeling that I wanted more; I wanted her to be real and to acknowledge her part in our relationship.

Following Ferenczi's emphasis on the empathic relationship between therapist and patient, Greenson (1981a) first attempted to define the dimensions of the realistic aspect of the therapy relationship. He noted that Ferenczi pointed to this concept when he described 'friendly relations which were based on reality and which proved to be viable'. Greenson (1981a) claimed that most analysts agree that there is transference and there is a real relationship, and it is important to distinguish between them. In fact, Greenson suggests that there is not a clear distinction between these aspects of the relationship. He stressed: 'All object relationships consist of different admixtures and blendings of real and transference components' (p. 89). He also made a distinction between the real relationship and the working alliance, and defined the real relationship as genuine and realistic. He suggested that, in contrast, the working alliance 'is essentially realistic; but more or less synthetic and artificial', although 'the reliable ending core of the working alliance is the "real relationship" between the patient and the analyst' (p. 95).

Greenson also asserted that the ability to form a real relationship with the analyst is the basis for deciding whether or not analysis can take place, whereas all patients will have transference reactions. He suggests that the aim of therapy is to replace the transference relationship with the real relationship. Finally, he claims that the importance of the real relationship implies a significant re-evaluation of the theory and technique of psychoanalysis. It would seem to be a consequence of this that the ability of the therapist to form a real relationship is an important basis for deciding whether or not analysis can take place. I can only conclude that my therapist was not able, or did not want, to form a real relationship with me.

Greenson (1981b) further considers the real relationship in 'Beyond transference and interpretation'. He suggests that the real relationship precedes and enables the resolution of the transference relationship. Greenson gives examples of real responsiveness from the analyst and of the analyst telling the patient how they affect the analyst. He suggests that examples of this real relationship should include 'spontaneous human reactions' (p. 99), acknowledging the importance of a patient's insights and apologising 'when your behaviour has been unnecessarily hurtful'. He also points to the oppressive power implications when the analyst does not respond in a real way, saying 'failure to be forthright in such matters injects an element of hypocrisy and oppressiveness in the analytic situation' (p. 100). He notes the element of protection for the therapist in using just a transference relationship when he suggests: 'we sometimes seem to use non-responsiveness and interpretations because they are safer and easier for us rather than best for the patient' (p. 100). However, he also points out the dangers in the real relationship of the patient believing this is an equal relationship. He suggests:

> It then becomes necessary to point out that, however equal we may be in certain ways . . . in the psychoanalytic situation he is the patient and the relatively unknowing and I am the expert, my errors notwithstanding. (p. 101)

Thus, it is clear that for Greenson the therapist defines the reality and 'knows' whether the patient needs a response from the real or the transference relationship.

Spinelli (1994) suggests that patients' reactions to the therapist are understandable in reaction to the therapist's behaviour, 'But by invoking terms such as transference, therapists are able to distance or exculpate themselves from such criticisms' (p. 186). He suggests that emotional reactions of the patient or therapist may have resonances with past relations, but are also meaningful of the current encounter. Thus, using the concept of transference means that 'the meaning of the emotional reaction within the current encounter is being minimised or obscured simply by imposing terms like transference or counter-transference on it' (p. 188). Instead, Spinelli suggests we consider that all encounters contain elements of transference and countertransference in that every encounter expresses similarities or resonances with previous experiences. However, he asserts that therapists need to 'engage with their clients and recognise that their presence is not only as a representative or transferential other, but that they are the other in the current encounter' (p. 193). This seems to echo the argument of Greenson (1981a, b). Spinelli argues that psychodynamic therapists will not let go of the notion of transference because of the illusion of expert knowledge that it entails: 'it is precisely the demystificatory nature of the suggestion which makes it so difficult for some therapists to consider it seriously' (1994, p. 190). Thus, the concept of transference provides a useful way for therapists to hold on to their expert power.

The lack of acknowledgement of a real relationship in my therapy certainly made me feel that there were oppressive power implications. I felt that I had no power to define my reality at all, and that any resistance to my therapist's definition would be interpreted and pathologised. It also seemed that my therapist's non-responsiveness did indeed offer her safety; I felt that she never risked being herself in our relationship. I acknowledge that this would have been a risk, both to her and to our therapy relationship, but for me as a patient, and now as a therapist, it is a risk worth taking.

My therapist seemed never to consider the possibility of using transference interpretations as a defence against emotions, and the number of times my feelings and behaviour were written off as 'resistance' were innumerable. She seemed completely impervious to criticism and reform. Maroda (1994) describes the defensive function of the abstinent and authoritarian stance for the therapist. She suggests that to respond in a 'real' way would put more demands on the therapist, who has difficulties tolerating emotions in the same way as patients do. She stresses that analysts will naturally avoid anything threatening their defences to keep what they want to remain hidden:

> What is distinctive about psychoanalysis is that the defences used by the therapist to protect himself are highly intellectualised and that this protection was built into the system at its conception. (p. 17)

Mahoney (1996) compares separate (objective) and connected (subjective) knowing in psychotherapy. 'Instead of looking for flaws, arguing and doubting, the connected knower and the connected therapist are predominantly empathic, exploratory and affirming' (p. 134). He suggests that connected knowing brings about healing, and is essential for the protection of the humanity of the patient. However, he again brings up the challenges for the therapist of this type of engagement with patients:

> I think it is important to acknowledge that there are emotional challenges to being connected and present as a psychotherapy practitioner. The more skilled one becomes in entering into the experiential worlds of one's clients, the more deeply one feels their struggles and suffering . . . These stories do not go away when the client does, they remain with us, haunting our dreams and popping up from time to time in our waking consciousness. (p. 141)

Maroda continues in this vein, saying:

> There is a fine line between using the intellect to organise emotional experience and to make it understandable, and using the intellect to defend against affect that is in some way threatening or undesirable. (1994, p. 17)

She also points out the difficulty of knowing when the former is slipping into the latter, especially when the patient's behaviour is all too often written off as resistance. This is another example of how psychoanalysis renders itself inscrutable and impervious to criticism, by interpreting any critical behaviour. Maroda emphasises the results of this: 'With this armament in place, psychoanalysis in many ways defies both criticism and reform' (1994, pp. 21–2).

Maroda suggests that the therapist can use the disclosure of countertransference feelings as a way of remaining in emotional contact with the patient (not distancing by intellectualising), but equally of not falling into the role the patient makes for the therapist. She clarifies: 'The idea is for therapists to respond to their patients' affect on a regular basis, rather than trying to remain impervious to them' (p. 27). She vehemently criticises the intellectualisation of interpretations:

> Why can the analytic therapist not acknowledge feeling, in addition to interpreting and offering intellectual understanding? To me, it defies reason that what is unquestionably an affective event, aimed at communication at an affective level, should ultimately be reduced to an intellectual statement, no matter how accurate that statement might be. (p. 30)

She further suggests the prime importance of emotions in therapy:

> We use our minds to defend against threatening thoughts, but simply put, our emotions do not lie. In this sense the emotional reality between therapist and patient is the only reality. (p. 31)

She equally stresses, however, that this mutually sharing relationship between therapist and patient is not equal:

> The therapist is responsible for being in control and preserving the necessary limits and restrictions on the constructively defined therapeutic relationship . . . Patients come to us because they believe we have sufficient knowledge, skill, and self-awareness to enable us to guide them through their own self-discovery. They rely on us to make the best decisions possible and to protect them from abuse and unnecessary pain as they make their journey. They give us power not to presume to know what is right for them but to listen to them, invite their co-operation, and then make the best decisions we possibly can about what is most therapeutic. (pp. 31–2)

I believe that this primacy of intellectual interpretations was probably counterproductive in my therapy, as one of the issues for me was of intellectualising everything and not allowing myself to feel. I suspect that this focus meant that at the very least the process of my becoming more able to feel took much longer than it might otherwise have done, or perhaps that therapy even impeded this process; that I grew *despite* therapy.

Taylor (1990) follows Szasz in suggesting that the idea of the authoritarian abstinent therapist protects the therapist. She explains that therapists being emotionally connected to patients carries the risk of pain and loss to the therapist. Thus traditional Freudian detachment also brings protection. She further explains that the conventional response of a psychodynamic therapist to the patient's questions, i.e. of exploring why the patient wants to know, 'leaves the person in therapy taking all the risks and the therapist in position of absolute power' (p. 116). She emphasises that most women have had too much emotional remoteness already, and that emotional connection in a therapy relationship is 'an integral part of the process of empowerment of women' (p. 116). Taylor (1990) also suggests that it is dishonest to pretend that the therapist can be neutral and that their behaviour could be unaffected by their values. She suggests that, to use psychodynamic therapy in a feminist way, the therapist must accept the concept of women's shared experiences while working towards a dynamic understanding of the woman patient's unique self. Also, by using the therapist's own feelings (the countertransference), the therapist can avoid objectifying the patient. Finally, 'In feminist therapy, there is no taboo on tenderness' (p. 117).

It seemed to me that my therapist was depersonalised in our relationship, and I felt deprived (of human contact and care). When I tried to tell her this, my memory is that she focused on interpreting why I believed she did not care because of my relationships in the past, and never on her way of behaving towards me, which contributed so much to my feelings. I can remember only one time when my therapist responded emotionally and really seemed to communicate from her own feelings, and thus conveyed warmth and care. My grandmother had just died and I had told her this and was upset. She said simply 'I'm sorry'. It felt as if she really meant it and cared about my distress. That one intervention has stayed in my mind. I still feel sad that this was the only time it happened, and regret that she might later have viewed this as a mistake, a relaxation of her boundaries. It seems tragic that if she did care she stopped herself communicating this, and I feel deprived of the care I could have received.

Clarkson (1992) illustrates a lesson she learned in practising psychodynamic counselling. She describes working in an 'abstinent' manner, and learning that 'We cannot live by analysis alone.' She explains that 'Early in my career . . . I persisted in working within the transference mode — at the expense of validating the personal humanity of the client with whom I was working' (p. 7). She notes that

> most people are so badly treated in their homes of origin in their
> childhood that they will tolerate a remarkable level of deprivation
> in psychotherapy or counselling because it is not as bad as what
> originally happened to them. (p. 7)

Clarkson describes how she finally managed to respond empathically and mutually to a patient who wanted to be touched. She emphasises the importance of this way of responding:

> The day she held out her hand again to me in a tentative,
> supplicating way, and I reached out to hold it in a simple, human,
> compassionate way, I truly learnt the value of person-to-person

relationship and the futility of applying prescriptions or proscriptions to the human spirit. She knew what she needed to be healed, which was subsequently borne out by her therapeutic progress — a human touch. I was moved by her and by her pain, and touched by her experience to feel an empathy that could only flower in human mutuality. (1992, p. 8)

Clarkson further adds her observation of the consequences for therapists of attempting to work following the 'rule of abstinence'. 'I have watched colleagues in protracted psychoanalysis become more depersonalised as they attempt to model themselves on the depersonalising analytic relationship.'

Maroda (1994) also criticises what she describes as the 'myth of authority'. She suggests that an authoritarian relationship only furthers the patient's psychopathology and that the therapy relationship should break the irrational tie to authority, rather than encourage it. Maroda also points to evidence that the neutral authoritarian stance may inhibit and distort the transference. She suggests that no stance can be genuinely neutral, and with an authoritarian stance, in which genuine exchanges with the therapist are not possible,

patients are more guarded and restrained, with the possible exception of frustration, rage and defences against these effects. The patient who never knows what his therapist really thinks is afraid of disapproval. (p. 15)

I never really knew what my therapist felt or thought about me, but the way everything was interpreted gave me the impression that I was disapproved of. I am sure part of this feeling was a transference reaction (and this of course was how it was interpreted), but again, its relevance to our real relationship, and her lack of communication of warmth or care, were consistently ignored and deflected.

I felt that my therapist's only goal was to develop my capacity to explore my ambivalent feelings about her, and she certainly made sure this was not foreclosed by a caring response. While totally abstaining from making any emotional responses in this process, she seems at the same time to have provided an environment that did not feel safe for me to be totally honest because of my fear of being blamed. Frosh (1997) considers the balance between the therapist providing a 'real' caring response to the patient and needing to encourage the patient's insight. He notes that patients need to develop the capacity to explore ambivalence, 'to recognise the way frustration of our desires provokes despair and hatred, and to find ways of understanding and working with this' (p. 110), which may be foreclosed by a therapist's caring response. Frosh (1997) suggests that the analytic process resides in the tension between 'being safe and being challenged, being looked after and being encouraged as an agent' (p. 111).

He similarly suggests the necessity of maintaining a balance of containment and pursuing insight through interpretation. With both these suggestions, he seems to be advocating a balance between the therapist acting in the transferential and the real relationships.

In focusing on the power of the therapist in the transference relationship, what can be missed is the power that is still present in the real relationship. Given that the level of power arising from the 'expert' position and authority of the therapist is reduced, there are still other aspects of power which are not considered. As the therapist is still in the role of authority, even speaking as a 'real' person or disclosing emotions is a powerful and potentially damaging — or helpful — intervention to make. In some of the literature in which the power in the transference relationship is criticised, it seems to be assumed that the 'real' relationship is bereft of inequalities of power, which is clearly not the case. Attention also needs to be paid to the ethical dilemmas involved in considering interventions in the 'real' relationship. (See also similar ethical dilemmas in self-disclosure in person-centred therapy in Chapter 6.)

Summary: power in the therapy relationship

My experiences of therapy, and my difficulties and discomfort with the relations of power that I experienced, demonstrate some fundamental issues in the practice of psychodynamic psychotherapy. Psychoanalytic discourse can have the effect of powerfully positioning the therapist as expert with armour to defend against all possible attacks. I was in a relatively privileged position with respect to education, knowledge and awareness about therapy when I began psychodynamic therapy, yet I struggled to challenge and leave the therapy relationship, and certainly struggled to hold on to my experiences. How much more difficult may this be for clients who are in much more powerless positions?

The critical literature on power in the psychoanalytic therapy relationship seems to be based on a concept of power that acknowledges the power of 'expertness', legitimised by science, and emphasises the link between power and knowledge. From this stance, it seems to be informed by post-structural concepts of power. However, the concept of power is still seen as unidirectional; the patient's contribution and resistance to the disciplinary power of the therapist (see Foucault and disciplinary power in Chapter 4) is not considered. Also, the power of the therapist is often seen as necessarily negative, although in the suggestions for the balance of the transference and real relationship there seems to be some suggestion that therapists could use their knowledge or experience in a positive way. However, this seems to be due more to a naïve conception that there is no power in the 'real' relationship.

Much has been written emphasising the power that can be abused in the transference relationship, and the possibility of minimising this power by paying equal attention to the real relationship between the therapist and patient, and exploring feelings associated with this that are experienced by both the therapist and the patient. A model of psychoanalytic therapy has recently been developed which takes this view of power very seriously and advocates the importance of the real relationship between therapist and patient. This model is the relational model, and it has been developed and used mainly in the USA.

The relational model of psychoanalysis

Aron (1996) espouses the relational model in detail and explains his understanding of mutuality in psychoanalysis. There were many contributions to the origins of this model. The earliest ideas were from Ferenczi's and Rank's contributions to the principles of mutuality and autonomy, which form the dialectic or tension that lies at the heart of relational psychoanalysis. Ferenczi and Rank also emphasised the therapy relationship and the reliving of affective experiences, in contrast to Freud's focus on intellectual understanding. Aron, too, notes the influences of object relations theorists, who moved the emphasis from drive theory to the drive to be in relationship. The British Independent school argued *for* the relational aspects of interpretation and *for* emotional responsiveness, and *against* the therapist's abstinence. The interpersonal tradition followed Ferenczi through Thompson, Sullivan and Fromm-Reichman, all moving in the direction of greater participation by the analyst, stressing the need for patients to know that they have affected the therapist. Aron also suggests that Buber's concept of intersubjectivity resonates with the relational approach. Finally, Kohut's emphasis on patients' resistances signalling a failure of empathy on the part of the therapist was another contribution to relational theory.

The key emphases in relational psychoanalysis are on intersubjectivity and mutuality. Instead of the therapist being in a position of authority to define reality, for relational psychoanalysts both the therapist and the patient have their own perspectives on the relationship which are equally valid. Here, the post-structuralist critiques of objectivity and the rationality of science are heeded (see Chapter 4). Neither pathology nor health lies exclusively in the patient or in the analyst; the analyst does not have a corner on truth: each have a valid perspective. In addition, rather than being a 'blank screen' or an object for the patient to project on to, in relational psychoanalysis the therapist is another subject whose subjectivity affects all aspects of the therapy encounter. Thus, transference is seen to be co-created by therapist and patient. Aron explains:

> Transference is not simply a distortion that emerges or unfolds from within the patient, independent of the actual behaviour or personality of the analyst. Rather the analyst is viewed as a participant in the

analysis whose behaviour has an interpersonal impact on the cocreation or coconstruction of the transference. (1996, p. 11)

Similarly, Aron stresses that transference and countertransference are bidirectional (although not equal) and mutual, continuous and ongoing, rather than occasional or intermittent. In fact, he suggests that the concept of intersubjectivity should replace the concepts of transference and countertransference, as it does not imply pathology, and does imply bidirectional and continuous influence. Here, post-structuralist concepts of mutual influence and the non-unidirectionality of power are evident (see Chapter 4). Similarly, Aron points out that 'Interpretations are always expressions of the analyst's subjectivity' (p. xiv). Later he further clarifies that all analysts' interventions are expressions of the analyst's subjectivity: there is no possible position of neutrality of objectivity. He emphasises

an understanding of interpretation as a mutual, intersubjective, affective, and interactive process . . . and interpersonal participation. It is an observation from within the interaction rather than outside it. (p. 118)

Thus, the interpretative process is reciprocal; resistances are mutual.

Objectivity is overturned with relational psychoanalysis, from the Freudian conception of psychoanalysis as archaeological reconstruction, to the idea of psychoanalysis as the active construction of a possible narrative guided by the theory of the analyst. The therapist's superior knowledge of the patient's psyche is abandoned in favour of a 'potential space' for a mutually creative construction of meaning. Thus, there is a revolutionary change in what the patient is presumed to need, from insight and a renunciation of infantile wishes (in the Freudian model), to the development of meaning and authenticity. The position of the analyst with respect to 'expert' knowledge and authority as critiqued by post-structuralist theories is overturned.

Along with the concept of intersubjectivity is the concept of subjectivity, of both the patient and the therapist, as including 'identity' and 'multiplicity'. Thus, 'intersubjective' implies relations among multiple personifications. Here, the post-structuralist insistence on the fragmented multiple subject is used. Intersubjectivity is explained as being always conflictual, as it is suggested that there are drives in each individual, both towards mutual recognition and a meeting of minds, and also to remain hidden. Aron describes the implications for the therapist of this conflict:

A dynamic tension needs to be preserved between responsiveness and participation, on one hand, and nonintrusiveness and space on the other, intermediate between the analyst's presence and absence. (1996, p. 87)

He further suggests that analysts are drawn to their profession because of their own conflicts over intimacy: 'Why else would anyone choose a profession in which one spends one's life listening and looking into the lives of others while one remains relatively silent and hidden' (p. 88).

Aron suggests that, since objectivity or 'correctness' is not a valid measure of the usefulness of an intervention, the usefulness of an intervention is due to its personal elements, the emotionally responsive aspects: 'It is through interpretations that the analyst best conveys his or her interest in, capacity to understand, and respect for the individuality of the patient' (p. 119). Further, 'People need to feel they are having an impact on others, and patients need to feel that they are having an emotional impact on their analysts' (p. 120).

This idea can be traced back to Ferenczi, who experimented with disclosing his own feelings to his patients. Ferenczi found that patients reacted to his passivity with increasing demands on his tolerance and patience, but when he expressed his feelings, a more real relationship developed in which his patients took account of the needs of others. Ferenczi also suggested that the Freudian 'neutral' position repeated the parenting experienced by traumatised patients. Aron (1996) explains that Ferenczi

> saw the polite aloofness of the analyst as a form of professional hypocrisy that kept both the patient's criticism of the analyst repressed and the analyst's true feelings towards the patient masked, although nevertheless felt by the patient. The analyst's emotional inaccessibility and insincerity repeated that of the traumatised patient's parents. (p. 163)

Ferenczi became increasingly convinced that the person of the analyst impacted on the patient. Aron summarises Ferenczi's legacy:

> Emotional honesty, accessibility, directness, openness, spontaneity, disclosure of the person of the analyst — these create in the patient heightened naturalness, forthrightness, access to the repressed, recognition of and sensitivity to the other, increased self-esteem, and greater realism about, and hence depth, in the relationship. (1996, p. 170)

Mutuality for Aron means sharing; this includes mutual data generation, mutual influence and mutual regulation. He stresses that mutual recognition is an aim, a developmental achievement, and that it will not be stable, but will itself be mutually regulated. He describes mutual recognition as recognition of each other's autonomy, and stresses that mutuality and autonomy are dialectical principles. He defines mutuality as authenticity and genuineness, an absence of pretence. He points out that an implication of the therapist's openness to their patient's perceptions of them, as another subject, is self-disclosure. However, he emphasises that 'self-revelation is not an option: it is an inevitability' (p. 84).

Throughout his description of the relational model, Aron is keen to emphasise that, although the therapy relationship is mutual, it is not equal. He points to the inevitability of the power differential in therapy explaining: 'My own position is that psychoanalysis is inevitably asymmetrical perhaps most importantly because there are differences in power between patient and analyst' (1996, p. 98). Again:

> Even while emphasising mutuality, however, one must keep in mind the important differences between patient and analyst in their roles, functions, power and responsibilities; this dimension of the relationship I refer to as asymmetry. (p. 124)

Aron also describes power as a changing dynamic between patient and analyst, and one that needs to be examined in therapy: 'Intimacy and collaboration are not easily achieved, because the patient and the analyst will exact power struggles between them that must be continually examined, articulated and worked through' (1996, p. 151). The main implication that Aron mentions of the asymmetrical relationship with respect to power is the therapist's responsibility that this entails. He suggests that the abandonment of objectivity does not necessitate the surrender of ethical standards, professional responsibility or clinical judgement. He asserts that the essence of asymmetry is that analysts must be responsible to accept their own subjectivity, which forms their clinical judgements; to continue to make choices, but to take responsibility for these choices based on their values. Therapists need to be aware of their own subjectivities and abilities to reflect on their participation in relationships, while recognising the limitations of their reflections. Here, unlike other literature, which assumes no power in the 'real' relationship, Aron acknowledges the inevitability of an unequal therapy relationship, and emphasises the importance of the therapist's responsibility to consider ethics.

Aron is here referring to two aspects of power in the therapy relationship. First, he considers aspects of *how* the therapist should be, and attempts to minimise the therapist's domination and authority over the patient by emphasising mutuality. But second, he also recognises that, however the therapist is in relation to the patient, they are still in the powerful role of therapist, and this entails a responsibility to examine their decisions with regard to ethics. In addition, therapists have a responsibility to consider their position in the context of their workplace and other expectations and demands on them. Aron recognises the power in the relationship arising from the personal histories of both the client and the therapist with respect to experiences of power, and, significantly, notes the importance of the therapist's history with his emphasis on mutuality. Thus, both the therapist and the patient are seen as important subjects in the power relation. The one aspect of the power relationship in therapy that he fails to consider is the structural positions of the therapist and the patient.

Benjamin (1988) emphasises the importance of intersubjectivity both in the therapy relationship and in all relationships, particularly parenting relationships; she advocates setting a model for relationships based on equality and negotiation rather than dominance and submission. She goes on to suggest that domination and submission are created from the transformed desire for recognition from another. If psychoanalysis includes the recognition of intersubjectivity, rather than that the therapist is the object for the patient, this will change the power dynamics involved, encouraging a more mutual and less authoritarian relationship.

Clinchy (1996) compares the idea of 'separate' knowing with the position of the analyst in Freudian psychoanalysis. She describes connected knowing, in contrast, as empathic, as trying to understand another's position, a 'bold swing . . . into the life of the other'. Clinchy suggests that connected knowing is moving beyond seeing the other as the viewer's object. She asks: 'How do we ensure that we are not merely treating the other as a mirror or a blot of ink, a mere receptacle for our own subjectivity?' (p. 220). She also points out the reciprocal process of connected knowing, the fact that connected knowing transforms the knower. This resonates with the hypothesis in relational psychoanalysis that therapy transforms both therapist and patient. Finally, she points to the mutual recognition involved in connected knowing, echoing Benjamin (1988). She agrees with Benjamin that

> connected knowing with the other and connected knowing with the self are reciprocal rather than oppositional processes: neither partner disappears into the other; each makes and keeps the other present. (1996, p. 232)

Summary

I have described psychodynamic therapy and some of the principles common to all models of psychoanalysis. I have also examined psychoanalytic theories of structural power, particularly with respect to gender relations. These point to the lack of questioning of the social construct of male supremacy and the ethnocentricity of classical theories of psychoanalysis. Obviously, theories based on these assumptions will have implications for the awareness of the structural positions of power of the therapist and patient in therapy. Considerations of structural power within psychoanalysis are generally explored from a more complex position than a radical environmental determinist position.[5] There is acknowledgement of the agency of subjects and the mutually determining effects of structures and agents. Understandings of internal psychic aspects of power relations are used to inform analysis of structural

---

5. A radical environmental determinist position asserts that individuals' levels of power are determined by their positions with regard to social structures. Power is seen as a possession.

positions, rather than reducing one to the other.

I have considered each aspect of the psychodynamic therapy relationship with respect to the power of the therapist. With regard to the transference relationship, I have emphasised the power invested in the therapist's ability to interpret the transference, and thus define reality. I criticised the model of the therapist as the objective expert. I considered and critiqued the 'working alliance'. Finally, I considered the 'real' relationship and the dangers in neglecting this. The real and transference aspects of the relationship both have implications for the power of the therapist in psychodynamic therapy, although there seems to be much greater potential for the abuse of power in the transference relationship. It is in the transference relationship that the therapist's authority, based on 'expert' knowledge, resides. However, I also noted that there is some questioning within psychoanalytic theory of an objective position arising from the notion of the dynamic unconscious. These competing constructs — of the therapist's 'expert knowledge' and the inability of anyone to 'know' — enable therapists to place themselves at varying points along a continuum regarding the status of the therapist's authority.

I have presented the relational model of psychoanalysis as a way forward to more seriously consider some of the aspects of power in the traditional psychodynamic relationship. It certainly challenges the power invested in the therapist in the transference relationship, and the position of the therapist to define the reality of the relationship. Other authors have demonstrated clearly the implications of the relational model and the idea of intersubjectivity on the dynamics of power in the therapy relationship.

However, Aron (1996) emphasises that, although the therapy relationship is mutual in relational psychoanalysis, it is still asymmetrical, and he warns that the implications of this asymmetry should not be neglected. Unfortunately, he says little about the implications of this asymmetry, although he suggests two ways for the therapist to minimise possible harm. First, analysts must be responsible for accepting their own subjectivity which forms clinical judgements; they should continue to make choices but need to take responsibility for these choices based on their values. Second, therapists need to be aware of their own subjectivities and their abilities to reflect on their participation in relationships while recognising the limitations of their reflections. Clearly, Aron is suggesting that therapists have a responsibility to examine their own position of power and to be responsible for their decisions and actions in therapy. However, it is not clear what decisions or actions would be considered harmful, or what might constitute positive uses of the therapist's power. However, Aron does explicitly consider two aspects of power in the therapy relationship: power in the role of the therapist ('*role power*'), and the personal histories of both the therapist and client ('*historical power*'). The only aspect he fails to consider is the structural aspects of power in the relationship ('*societal power*'). To seriously consider the inequality in the therapy relationship, it is essential that the therapist consider the effects of structural positions.

Chapter 8

Conclusions: so what can we do about power?

Each of the models of therapy I have considered, and probably all models of therapy, work with the implicit assumption that mental well-being is associated with a feeling of control and power over one's life. It is generally accepted that experiencing and feeling powerless is associated with psychological distress. The questions are: How can therapy best empower the client? Does the power inherent in the therapy relationship hinder this, and if so, how can this effect be ameliorated? Read and Wallcraft (1992) define empowerment as follows: 'No one can give power to another person but they can stop taking their power away. They can also help people to regain their own power.' Empowerment goes beyond the interpersonal therapy relationship and connects with the much wider political environment. However, the distribution of power in the therapy relationship is a very important template for the distribution of power in the wider context.

Summary

Three aspects of power in the therapy relationship have been considered: the power arising from the roles of therapist and client (*role power*), the power arising from the structural positions of therapist and client (*societal power*), and the power arising from the personal histories of therapist and client with respect to experiences of power and powerlessness (*historical power*). I have presented the literature on power in therapy and have argued that the majority of this literature is based implicitly on structural models of power. Thus, the literature assumes that power is unidirectional, is a possession, is monolithic and is necessarily negative. I have also presented post-structural concepts of power, arguing that these concepts of power broaden our understanding of power in the therapy relationship by enabling us to see power: as something that is present in the relationship rather than being the possession of one person; as bidirectional and influenced also by outside relationships; as inescapable, and as potentially both negative and positive.

I have discussed three different models of therapy and pointed out the gaps in the analyses of power within these models. *Cognitive behaviour therapy* (CBT) fails to analyse and problematise the position of the therapist as expert, as 'objective scientist', and thus is at risk of abusing a position of power, while obscuring the therapist's powerful position within the rhetoric of 'collaboration'. It fails to address any of the three aspects of power in the therapy relationship, primarily because of its lack of focus on the therapy relationship per se.

Person-centred therapy (PCT) addresses all aspects of power in the therapy relationship. This theory provides a radical alternative to the dominant medical model of the 'ill' and untrustworthy client. The PCT relationship is set up to reduce the potential for domination and control by the therapist. However, sometimes the focus on the therapist as a person is in danger of obscuring the power inherent in the role of therapist, and there is potential for therapists to miss levels of oppression resulting from structural positions unless the socially positioned person is acknowledged.

Psychodynamic therapy has addressed some issues of power in the relationship by examining the various aspects of the therapy relationship. I have presented the model of relational psychoanalysis, which tackles most aspects of power in the relationship and aims to protect the client from domination and the therapist's authority. Psychodynamic therapists can fall along a continuum of how much they use the real relationship to address issues of power in the transference relationship, and how much they acknowledge the limitations of the therapist's authority because of a lack of objectivity in perceiving a dynamic unconscious.

In both person-centred therapy and psychodynamic therapy, where *role power* is considered, mutuality in the therapy relationship is promoted. This concept is referred to in several ways, using Buber's concept of I-thou relations, the person-centred concept of a person-to-person relationship, the idea of connected knowing, or the psychoanalytic term of 'mutuality'. In all these concepts the therapist's authority is questioned, with the emphasis on the therapist's own subjectivity, and the client's view is emphasised. The importance of the therapist's openness and 'realness' is stressed. The acknowledgement of the therapist's authority based on their role is acknowledged to be inescapable, and the necessity of considering the responsibility for using this power positively is highlighted.

In considering *societal power*, recommendations are made for considering the socially positioned individual, in order to acknowledge structural positions in society, while noting the interaction with individual subjectivity and agency.

Both psychoanalytic and person-centred models of therapy theorise *historical power*. Integral to the analysis of this aspect of power is the emphasis on self-awareness for the therapist and on supervision as a check on the therapist's feelings and motives for their behaviour in therapy.

Themes

The following themes recur throughout this book and summarise the conclusions drawn:

1. Power is dynamic and relational. The dynamics of power in relationships are ever changing and are constantly to be explored.
2. Power is ubiquitous. The dynamics of power are in every relationship and cannot be dissolved in a utopia of transparency.
3. Post-structural concepts of power remind us that all subjects have agency and that there is resistance to the operations of power. However, structural theories of power remind us that the effectiveness of resistance is determined partly by structural positions. It is essential that resistance is not used to justify oppression and domination.
4. Three types of power to consider are *power-over*, *power-from-within* and *power-with*. The aim in exploring dynamics of power is not to erase or obscure power, but to minimise the negative aspects (particularly domination) and to maximise the positives (such as collective power and using power to resist structures of domination and to maximise the *power-from-within* of both the client and therapist).

A way forward

It is rare to find discussions about power that do not rely on structural models of power as monolithic, unidirectional and necessarily negative. Either power is ignored, concealed by rhetoric of equality or collaboration; or, at the other extreme, using structural models of power leads to a radical environmentalist behaviourism, suggesting a treatment of people as 'black boxes', as 'docile bodies' upon whom structural forces act. The challenge for therapists is to take seriously issues of power in all their complexity without reducing all these aspects and complex dynamics between people to obscure either structures or individual agency. Of course, theoretically, balancing these concepts requires a multidisciplinary approach. It means that psychology, counselling and therapy training must take seriously what has been discovered and explored by sociologists, political theorists and philosophers.

Issues of power raise ethical questions, and values are an inescapable part of the consideration of power. In codes of practice for therapy — the ethical codes of beneficence and non-maleficence — are clear, although the balance between this and autonomy is left to decisions by individuals. Heath (1992) suggests that our need to believe in benevolent intention prevents us addressing issues of misuse of power. However, it is clear in the aims of therapy that we are to try to help clients take more control of their lives. We need to consider carefully how our roles as therapists help or hinder this aim, particularly with respect to the internal consistency of the means and the end. If we take control, and do not think carefully how to avoid domination during therapy, how can we expect clients to walk away feeling more in control?

Both psychodynamic therapy and PCT provide ideas and ways for therapists to consider responsibly the issues of power that are summarised above. CBT is far behind with respect to this issue at the moment, and seems to be prevented from taking serious consideration of the issues by the myth of the objective scientist and expert and by the lack of consideration about the therapy relationship. As CBT is the main model advocated by clinical psychologists in the UK, if clinical psychologists wish to be taken seriously in their work as therapists, they need to develop a clear model of ethical behaviour and values underpinning their work, to challenge or supplement the scientist practitioner model.

Checklist for consideration of power in therapy

Whatever model of therapy is being used, this book should provide a framework to enable its practitioners to analyse and explore the dynamics of power in therapy. The following checklist summarises how it would be useful to analyse power in therapy.

1. Consider each of the three aspects of power in the therapy relationship:

   (a) Role power. This refers to the power arising from the roles of therapist and client. The therapist would best inform their analysis of this by listening to what people who have been clients of therapists say about the roles with regard to power. There is now much literature addressing this issue from the service user movement concerning therapy (e.g. Ward, 1993). Therapists need generally to examine their model of therapy and the position this places them in with respect to power and their attitude to the client's autonomy. How does the therapist conceptualise their position in terms of expertness, responsibility? (See Johnstone, 1989.) How does this translate into the therapist's attitude towards the client? Then, with each client, the therapist can also consider the client's position and attitude towards their own role and towards the therapist's role. How does the client see themselves? Do they see the therapist as the expert? How clear has the therapist been about what they can provide and their own limitations? Has the therapist been clear about their own ethical position (particularly with regard to autonomy or beneficence)? Has the client had a choice to work with someone using a different approach or for this therapist to take a different approach?

(b) Societal power. This refers to the power arising from the structural positions of therapist and client. Awareness of the social and political context is essential for therapists to consider the socially positioned individual, and to address the interaction of the individual with their environment and to avoid pathologising the individual. In particular, the social causes of distress need to be considered and understood. For therapists to consider this issue with each client, it is essential that they have already explored their own structural positions with regard to power and oppression and the effect of these positions on themselves and others in relationships. Then with each particular client the structural positions of the client can be considered, although it is important not to make assumptions about which positions clients hold or how those positions affect them. However, it is useful to be aware of the structural positions of power held by therapist and client in relation to one another, which can magnify the inequality set up by the power in the roles of therapist and client. For example, for a middle-class therapist working with a working-class client, it is not possible to assume the attitudes of the client towards a middle-class professional purely from their working-class identity. However, an awareness of these positions and the history and current manifestations of class oppression will enable the therapist to be open to considering the positions, attitudes and differences within that individual relationship. Attenborough et al. (2000) stress the necessity for therapists to be aware of the social and political context and suggest areas that need to be considered. Williams and Watson (1994) suggest a checklist for therapists learning about the effects of social inequalities on the lives of women, which includes learning from women service users, from theory and research, from women-centred mental health projects and from our own experience of power and powerlessness. A similar checklist can be devised for each social inequality.

(c) Historical power. This refers to the power arising from the personal histories of therapist and client with respect to experiences of power and powerlessness. Again, awareness of this aspect of power requires therapists to be aware of their own history and experiences and how it affected them. This could include an awareness of particular dynamics in relationships that trigger certain responses in the therapist with respect to feeling powerless or powerful. Particularly important would be an awareness of triggers that may provoke feelings of powerlessness in the therapist and lead the therapist to react by exerting power over the client to try to regain their own sense of power. Awareness of the power arising from the personal history of the client will lead to a gradual understanding between therapist and client of these issues as the client discloses more about their life. It would also be useful for the therapist to

have an awareness of some general issues in terms of the likely effects of particular experiences, for example the possible effects of experiencing childhood sexual abuse, on a survivor's sense of power or powerlessness. Again, as with structural positions, it is essential that these generalisations are not used to assume particular issues with any individual, but that, by being aware of the possibility, the therapist is open to considering the dynamics with a particular individual.

2. Cromwell and Olson's (1975) domains of power
Another useful way to conceptualise practically the relations of power in the therapy dyad is to consider Cromwell and Olson's (1975) domains of power. They conceptualise power in families as a construct incorporating three analytically distinct but interrelating domains: power bases, power processes and power outcomes. *Power bases* are the economic and personal assets (such as income, economic independence, control of surplus money, sex-role attitudes, desire for intimacy, physical and psychological aggression) that form the basis of one partner's control over the other. *Power processes* are interactional techniques, such as persuasion, problem-solving or demandingness, that individuals use in their attempts to gain control over aspects of the relationship. *Power outcomes* determine who has the final say — who determines the outcome in problem-solving or decision-making. *Power bases* comprise of all the above three aspects of power. Additional useful ways to analyse power in practice involve the consideration of *power processes*, which could be useful to analyse in the interaction within therapy, a way to consider Foucault's idea of 'normalising discourses'. *Power outcomes* are a final analysis in practice of the reality of power in therapy; however collaborative a therapist purports to be, if the therapist still determines the outcome in decision-making, the 'collaborative process' taken to arrive at that point is a nonsense.

Politics

This book has considered power relations in the therapy dyad, purely from within the therapy relationship. However, there are also power relations in institutions and on a political level that affect the therapy relationship. An example is the institutional homophobia in psychoanalysis. In addition to an analysis of power relations on the micro level within the therapy relationship, an analysis of political levels of power is also necessary, and political resistance is necessary. On this level, democratic debate, transparency and the enhancement of the rights of clients to object and litigate all contribute to the analysis and changing of damaging power relations.

On a more personal level, Foucault's ethics of scepticism and constant questioning is a necessary and useful attitude to take to the ethics of power in therapy. We need to question each time we come across anything that seems to be self-evident to free up knowledge and open up new possibilities for thought or action. Here we can learn from the service user movement and its questioning of so many principles within mental health that have been taken for granted for far too long. This means being constantly aware and watchful. As Foucault (1984) stresses, 'Problematisation and apprehension go hand in hand; inquiry is joined to vigilance' (p. 239).

Resistance and change can occur at several levels. Political resistance can challenge and change institutions and make a difference at structural levels of power. Research and theory can inform and continue the democratic debate and bring power relations out into an open arena. Resistance at the level of practice, by analysing and changing the practices of individual clinicians, not only changes and challenges within particular therapy relationships, but also contributes to more pervasive changes in theory.

References

Adcock, C. and Newbigging, K. (1990). Women in the shadows: women, feminism and clinical psychology. In E. Burman (ed.), *Feminist Psychology* (pp. 172–188). London: Sage.

Allison, A. (1996). A framework for good practice: ethical issues in cognitive behaviour therapy. In S. Marshall and J. Turnbull (eds.), *Cognitive Behaviour Therapy* (pp. 155–180). London: Balliere Tindall.

Archer, M. (1995). *Realist Social Theory: The morphogenetic approach.* Cambridge: Cambridge University Press.

Arendt, H. (1963). *On Revolution.* London: Penguin.

Arendt, H. (1986). Communicative power. In S. Lukes (ed.), *Power* (pp. 61–74). Oxford: Basil Blackwell.

Arnold, L. and Magill, A. (1998). *The Self-harm Help Book.* Abergavenny: The Basement Project.

Aron, L. (1996). *A Meeting of Minds.* London: Analytic Press.

Attenborough, L., Hawkins, J., O'Driscoll, D. and Proctor, G. (2000). Clinical psychology in context: the impact of the socio-political environment. *Clinical Psychology Forum,* 142: 13–17.

Baker Miller, J.(1976). *Towards a New Psychology of Women.* New York: Beacon Press.

Baker Miller, J.(1991). The development of a woman's sense of self. In J. Jordan, A. Kaplan, J. Baker Miller, I. Stiver and J. Surrey (eds.), *Women's Growth in Connection* (pp. 11–26). London: Guildford Press.

Bannister, D. (1983). The internal politics of psychotherapy. In D. Pilgrim (ed.), *Psychology and Psychotherapy: Current trends and issues.* London: Routledge & Kegan Paul.

Beck, A. T. (1976). *Cognitive Therapy and Emotional Disorders.* New York: International University Press.

Beck, A. T., Rush, A. T., Shaw, B. F. and Emery, G. (1979). *Cognitive Therapy of Depression.* New York: Guildford Press.

Beetham, D. (1996). *Bureaucracy.* Milton Keynes: Open University Press.

Benjamin, J. (1988). *The Bonds of Love: Psychoanalysis, feminism, and the problem of domination.* New York: Virago.

Binnett, E., Dennis, M., Dosanjh, N., Mahtani, A., Miller, A., Nadirshaw, Z. and Patel, N. (1995). Race and culture resource pack for trainers. Training Working Party, Division of Clinical Psychology, British Psychological Society.

Bostock, J. (1998). From clinic to community: generating social validity in clinical psychology. *Clinical Psychology Forum,* 121: 2–6.

Bozarth, J. (1998). *Person-Centred Therapy: A revolutionary paradigm.* Ross-on-Wye: PCCS Books.

Bracken, P. and Thomas, P. (2001). Postpsychiatry: a new direction for mental health. *British Medical Journal,* 32: 724–727.

Breggin, P. (1993). *Toxic Psychiatry.* London: Harper Collins.

Brink, D. (1987). The issues of equality and control in the client or person-centred approach. *Journal of Humanistic Psychotherapy*, 27: 27–38.

Brodley, B. T. (1997). The nondirective attitude in client-centered therapy. *The Person-Centered Journal*, 4 (1): 18–30.

Brodley, B. T. (1999). Reasons for responses expressing the therapist's frame of reference in client-centered therapy. *The Person-Centered Journal*, 6 (1): 4–27.

Brown, S. W. and Harris, T. (1978). *Social Origins of Depression: A study of psychiatric disorder in women*. London: Tavistock.

Buber, M. (1970). *I and Thou*. Edinburgh: T. & T. Clarke Ltd (trans. W. Kaufman).

Burns, D. and Auerbach, A. (1996). Therapeutic empathy in cognitive behavioural therapy: does it really make a difference? In P. Salkovskis (ed.), *Frontiers of Cognitive Therapy* (pp. 135–64). New York: Guildford Press.

Burstow, B. (1987). Humanistic psychotherapy and the issue of equality. *Journal of Humanistic Psychotherapy*, 27: 9–25.

Butler, J. (1990). *Gender Trouble: Feminism and the subversion of identity*. London: Routledge.

Butler, J. (1992). Contingent foundations: feminism and the question of 'postmodernism'. In J. Butler and J. Scott (eds.), *Feminists theorise the Political* (pp. 3–21). London: Routledge.

Butler, J. (1997). *The Psychic Life of Power*. Stanford, CA: Stanford University Press.

Byrne, M. and Carr, A. (2000). Depression and power in marriage. *Journal of Family Therapy*, 22: 408–27.

Chesler, P. (1972). *Women and Madness*. New York: Doubleday.

Clarkson, P. (1992). We cannot live by analysis alone. In W. Dryden (ed.), *Hard-earned Lessons from Counselling in Action*. London: Sage.

Clegg, J. S. (1989). *Frameworks of Power*. London: Sage.

Clements, J. and Rapley, M. (1996). Go to the mirror! *Clinical Psychology Forum*, 89: 4–7.

Clinchy, B. (1996). Connected and separate knowing. In N. Goldberger, J. Tarule, B. Clinchy, and M. Belenky (eds.), *Knowledge, Difference and Power* (pp. 205–47). New York: Basic Books.

Cooke, M. and Kipnis, D. (1986). Influence tactics in psychotherapy. *Journal of Consulting and Clinical Psychology*, 54: 22–6.

Cooper, D. (1967). *Psychiatry and Anti-Psychiatry*. London: Tavistock.

Cousins, M. and Hussein, A. (1984). *Michel Foucault*. London: Macmillan Education Ltd.

Cromwell, R. E. and Olson, D. H. (1975). *Power in Families*. New York: John Wiley.

Darongkamas, J., Burton, M. and Cushway, D. (1994). The use of personal therapy by clinical psychologists working in the NHS in the United Kingdom. *Clinical Psychology and Psychotherapy*, 1(3): 165–73.

Daudi, P. (1986). *Power in the Organisation: The discourse of power in managerial praxis*. Oxford: Basil Blackwell.

Deleuze, G. and Guattari, F. (1984). *Anti-Oedipus: Capitalism and schizophrenia*. London: Athlone Press.

DeVaris, J. (1994). The dynamics of power in psychotherapy. *Psychotherapy*, 31: 588–93.

Elshtain, J. (1992). The power and powerlessness of women. In Bock, G. and James, S. (eds.), *Beyond Equality and Difference: Citizenship, feminist politics and female subjectivity*. London: Routledge.

Fanon, F. (1986). *Black Skin, White Masks*. London: Pluto Press.

Farrington, A. and Telford, A. (1996). Naming the problem: assessment and formulation. In S. Marshall and J. Turnbull (eds.), *Cognitive Behaviour Therapy* (pp. 57–90). London: Balliere Tindall.

Fernando, S. (1991). *Mental Health, Race and Culture*. London: Macmillan/MIND.

Finkelhor, D. (1986). *A Sourcebook on Child Sexual Abuse*. London: Sage.

Fish, V. (1999). Clementis's Hat: Foucault and the politics of psychotherapy. In I. Parker (ed.), *Deconstructing Psychotherapy* (pp. 54–70). London: Sage.

Foucault, M. (1977). *Discipline and Punish*. London: Penguin Press.

Foucault, M. (1977). *Madness and Civilisation*. London: Tavistock.

Foucault, M. (1980). *Power and Knowledge: Selected interviews and other writings 1972–1977*. Brighton: Harvester Press.

Foucault, M. (1981). *The History of Sexuality,* Vol. 1. Harmondsworth: Penguin.

Foucault, M. (1984). *The History of Sexuality,* Vol. 3: *The Care of the Self.* London: Penguin.

French, M. (1985). *Beyond Power: On women, men and morals.* London: Jonathan Cape.

Frosh, S. (1997). *For and Against Psychoanalysis.* London: Routledge.

Garrett, T. and Davis, J. (1995). So who are we anyway? *Clinical Psychology Forum,* 78: 2–4.

Gilbert, P. (1992). *Depression: The evolution of powerlessness.* Hove, Sussex: Lawrence Erlbaum Associates.

Goffman, E. (1963). *Stigma: Notes on the management of a spoiled identity.* London: Penguin.

Gomm, R. (1996). Mental health and inequality. In T. Heller, J. Reynolds, R. Gomm, R. Muston, and S. Pattison (eds.), *Mental Health Matters: A reader.* London: Macmillan in association with the Open University.

Grant, B. (1990). Principled and instrumental non-directiveness in person-centred and client-centred therapy. *Person-centred Review,* 5: 77–88.

Greenson, R. (1981a). The real relationship between the patient and psychoanalyst. In R. Langs (ed.), *Classics in Psychoanalytic Technique.* NY, USA and London: Aronson.

Greenson, R. (1981b). Beyond transference and interpretation. In R. Langs (ed.), *Classics in Psychoanalytic Technique.* NY, USA and London: Aronson.

Grimshaw, J. (1993). Practices of freedom. In C. Ramazanoglu (ed.), *Up Against Foucault: Explorations of some tensions between Foucault and feminism* (pp. 51–72). London: Routledge.

Grostein, J. (1990). The contribution of attachment theory and self-regulation theory to the therapeutic alliance. *Modern Psychoanalysis,* 15: 169–84.

Haworth, R. (1998). Mental health professionals' accounts of clients who are from ethnic minorities. *Clinical Psychology Forum,* 118: 6–10.

Hawton, K., Salkovskis, P., Kirk, J. and Clark, D. (1989). *Cognitive Behaviour Therapy for Psychiatric Problems.* Oxford: Oxford University Press.

Heath, G. (1992). Is there therapy after Masson? *Clinical Psychology Forum,* 45, 32–6.

Hinshelwood, R. D. (1997). *Therapy or Coercion? Does psychoanalysis differ from brainwashing?* London: Karnac Books.

Humm, M. (1992). *Feminisms: A reader.* London: Harvester Wheatsheaf.

Hurvitz, N. (1973). Psychotherapy as a means of social control. *Journal of Consulting and Clinical Psychology,* 40: 232–239.

Jacobs, M. (1988). *Psychodynamic Counselling in Action.* London: Sage.

Johnstone, L. (1989). *Users and Abusers of Psychiatry.* London: Routledge.

Johnstone, L. (1997). 'I hear what you're saying': How to avoid jargon in therapy. *Changes,* 15 (4): 264–270.

Johnstone, L. (1999). Do families cause 'schizophrenia'? Revisiting a taboo subject. In C. Newnes, G. Holmes, and C. Dunn (eds.), *This is Madness: A critical look at psychiatry and the future of mental health services* (pp. 119–34). Ross-on-Wye: PCCS Books.

Katzman, M. (1997). Getting the difference right: It's power not gender that matters. *European Eating Disorders Review,* 5: 71–4.

Kearney, A. (1996). *Counselling, Class and Politics: Undeclared influences in therapy.* Manchester: PCCS Books.

Kipnis, D. (1976). *The Powerholders.* Chicago/London: University of Chicago Press.

Kirk, J. (1989). Cognitive behavioural assessment. In K. Hawton, P. Salkovskis, J. Kirk and D. M. Clark (eds.), *Cognitive Behaviour Therapy for Psychiatric Problems* (pp. 13–51). Oxford: Oxford University Press.

Kirschenbaum, H. and Henderson, V.L. (Eds)(1989) *The Carl Rogers Reader.* Boston: Houghton Mifflin.

Kitzinger, C. and Perkins, R. (1993). *Changing our Minds: Lesbian feminism and psychology.* London: Onlywomen Press.

Laing, R. D. (1985). *Wisdom, Madness and Folly.* London: Macmillan.

Larner, G. (1999). Derrida and the deconstruction of power as context and topic in therapy. In I. Parker (ed.), *Deconstructing Psychotherapy* (pp. 39–53). London: Sage.

Law, I. (1999). A discursive approach to therapy with men. In I. Parker (ed.), *Deconstructing Psychotherapy* (pp. 115–31). London: Sage.

Lowe, R. (1999). Between the 'No longer' and the 'Not yet': postmodernism as a context for critical therapeutic work. In I. Parker (ed.), *Deconstructing Psychotherapy* (pp. 71–85). London: Sage.

Lukes, S. (1974). *Power: A radical view.* London: Macmillan.

Lukes, S. (1986). *Power.* Oxford: Basil Blackwell.

Madigan, S. (1999). Inscription, description and deciphering chronic identities. In I. Parker (ed.), *Deconstructing Psychotherapy* (pp. 150–63). London: Sage.

Maguire, M. (1995). *Men, Women, Passion and Power: Gender issues in psychotherapy.* London: Routledge.

Mahoney, M. (1996). Connected knowing in constructive psychotherapy. In N. Goldberger, J. Tarule, B. Clinchy and M. Belenky (eds.), *Knowledge, Difference and Power* (pp. 126–47). New York: Basic Books.

Malan, D. (1979). *Individual Psychotherapy and the Science of Psychodynamics.* Oxford: Butterworth Heinemann.

Maroda, K. (1994). *The Power of Countertransference.* London: Aronson.

Marshall, S. (1996). The characteristics of cognitive behaviour therapy. In S. Marshall and J. Turnbull (eds.), *Cognitive Behaviour Therapy* (pp. 29–54). London: Balliere Tindall.

Marshall, S. and Turnbull, J. (eds.) (1996). *Cognitive Behaviour Therapy.* London: Balliere Tindall.

Masson, J. (1989). *Against Therapy.* London: Fontana.

McNay, L. (1992). *Foucault and Feminism: Power, gender and the self.* Cambridge: Polity Press.

Meichenbaum, D. (1977). *Behaviour Modification: An integrative approach.* New York: Plenum Press.

Mercer, K. (1986). Racism and transcultural psychiatry. In P. Miller and N. Rose (eds.), *The Power of Psychiatry* (pp. 112–42). Cambridge: Polity Press.

Miller, P. and Rose, N. (1986). Introduction (Miller and Rose) and Chapter 1 (Miller), 'Critiques of psychiatry and critical sociologies of madness'. In P. Miller and N. Rose (eds.), *The Power of Psychiatry.* Cambridge: Polity Press.

Natiello, P. (2001) *The PersonCentered Approach: A passionate presence.* Ross-on-Wye. PCCS Books.

Newnes, C. and Holmes, G. (1999). The future of mental health services. In C. Newnes, G. Holmes and C. Dunn (eds.), *This is Madness: A critical look at psychiatry and the future of mental health services* (pp. 273–84). Ross-on-Wye: PCCS Books.

Nietzsche, F. (1969). *On the Genealogy of Morals.* New York: Vintage Books.

Nietzsche, F. (1977). *A Nietzsche Reader.* London: Penguin.

O'Reilly Byrne, N. and Colgan McCarthy, I. (1999). Feminism, politics and power in therapeutic discourse: fragments from the Fifth Province. In I. Parker (ed.), *Deconstructing Psychotherapy* (pp. 86–102). London: Sage.

O'Reilly, P. (1983). Personal psychology and the therapy of families. In D. Pilgrim (ed.), *Psychology and Psychotherapy: Current trends and issues.* London: Routledge & Kegan Paul.

Parker, I. (1999). Deconstruction and psychotherapy. In I. Parker (ed.), *Deconstructing Psychotherapy* (pp. 1–18). London: Sage.

Pilgrim, D. (1983). Politics, Psychology and Psychiatry. In D. Pilgrim (ed.), *Psychology and Psychotherapy: Current Trends and Issues* (pp. 121–38). London: Routledge & Kegan Paul.

Pilgrim, D. (1997). *Psychotherapy and Society.* London: Sage.

Pilgrim, D. and Treacher, A. (1992). *Clinical Psychology Observed.* London: Routledge.

Proctor, G. (1994). Lesbian clients' experience of clinical psychology: a listener's guide. *Changes,* 12: 290–8.

Rajchman, J. (1985). *Michel Foucault: The freedom of philosophy.* New York: Columbia University Press.

Ransome, P. (1992). *Antonio Gramsci: A new introduction.* London: Harvester Wheatsheaf.

Read, J. and Wallcraft, J. (1992). *Guidelines for Empowering Users of Mental Health Services.* London: MIND Publications and COHSE (Confederation of Health Service Employees).

Riikonen, E. and Vataja, S. (1999). Can (and should) we know how, where and when psychotherapy takes place? In I. Parker (ed.), *Deconstructing Psychotherapy* (pp. 175–188). London: Sage.

Rogers, C.R. (1957). The necessary and sufficient conditions for therapeutic personality change. *Journal of Consulting Psychology,* 21: 95–103.

Rogers, C.R. (1959). A theory of therapy, personality and interpersonal relationships as developed in the client-centered framework. In S. Koch (ed.), *Psychology: A study of a science,* Vol. III: *Formulations of the Person and the Social Context* (pp. 184–256) New York and London: McGraw-Hill.

Rogers, C.R. (1978a). *Carl Rogers on Personal Power.* London: Constable.

Rogers, C.R. (1978b). My political view. Statement made to the El Escorial workshop, March 31. Unpublished manuscript.

Rose, N. (1985). *The Psychological Complex.* London: Routledge & Kegan Paul.

Rowan, J. (1994). Therapy for the therapists. *Self and Society,* 22(5): 23.

Rowe, D. (1989). Foreword. In J. Masson (ed.), *Against Therapy.* London: Fontana.

Rutter, M. (1990). Psychosocial resilience and protective mechanisms. In J. Rolf, A. Masten, D. Cicchetti, K. Neuchterlain and S. Weintraub (eds.), *Risk and Protective Factors in the Development of Psychopathology* (pp. 181–214). New York: Cambridge University Press.

Sainsbury Centre for Mental Health (1997). *Pulling Together: The future roles and training of mental health staff.* London: Sainsbury Centre for Mental Health.

Sampson, R.V. (1965). *The Psychology of Power.* New York: Vintage Books.

Sanders, P. and Tudor, K. (2001). This is therapy: a person-centred critique of the contemporary psychiatric system. In C. Newnes, G. Holmes and C. Dunn (eds.), *This is Madness Too: Critical perspectives on mental health services* (pp. 147–60). Ross-on-Wye: PCCS Books.

Sandler, J. Dare, C. and Holder, A. (1992). *The Patient and the Analyst.* London: Karnac Books.

Sayers, J. (1986). *Sexual Contradictions: Psychology, psychoanalysis and feminism.* London: Tavistock.

Schaap, C., Bennun, I., Schindler, L. and Hoogduin, K. (1993). *The Therapeutic Relationship in Behavioural Psychotherapy.* Chichester: John Wiley.

Schwaber, E. (1983). Psychoanalytic listening and psychic reality. *International Review of Psychoanalysis,* 10, 379–92.

Searle, Y. (1993). Ethical issues within the therapeutic relationship: autonomy or paternalism? *Clinical Psychology Forum,* 60, 31–6.

Seligman, M. E. P. (1974). Depression and learned helplessness. In R. J. Friedman and M. M. Katz (eds.), *The Psychology of Depression: Contemporary theory and research.* Washington DC: Winston.

Sherrard, C. (1999). Pseudo-symmetry: novel linguistic forms in clinical psychologists' writing. Paper presented at the 18th International Human Science Research Conference, Sheffield.

Shlien, J.M. (1984). A countertheory of transference. In R. Levant and J. Shlien (eds.) *Client Centered Therapy and the Person Centered Approach*. New York: Praeger.

Smail, D. (1987). Psychotherapy as subversion in a make-believe world. *Changes*, 4(5): 398–402.

Smail, D. (1995). Power and the origins of unhappiness: working with individuals. *Journal of Community and Applied Social Psychology*, 5: 347–356.

Smart, B. (1985). *Michel Foucault*. Chichester: Ellis Horwood.

Spandler, H. (1996). *Who's Hurting Who? Young people, self-harm and suicide*. Manchester: 42nd Street.

Spinelli, E. D. (1994). *Demystifying Therapy*. London: Constable.

Spinelli, E. D. (1998). Counselling and the abuse of power. *Counselling*, 9 (3), 181–4.

Starhawk (1987). *Truth or Dare: Encounters with Power, Authority, and Mystery*. San Francisco: Harper & Row.

Sterba, R. (1981). The fate of the ego in analytic therapy. In R. Langs (ed.), *Classics in Psychoanalytic Technique*. NY, USA and London: Aronson.

Swan, V. (1999). Narrative, Foucault and feminism: implications for therapeutic practice. In I. Parker (ed.), *Deconstructing Psychotherapy* (pp. 103–14). London: Sage.

Szasz, T. (1963). The concept of transference. *International Journal of Psychoanalysis*, 44: 432–43.

Szasz, T. (1997, first published 1970). *The Manufacture of Madness: A comparative study of the Inquisition and the mental health movement*. Syracuse, NY: Syracuse University Press.

Taylor, M. (1990). Fantasy or reality? The problem with psychoanalytic interpretation in psychotherapy with women. In E. Burman (ed.), *Feminists in Psychological Practice* (pp. 104–18). London: Sage.

Telford, A. and Farrington, A. (1996). Handing over: generalisation and maintenance of self-management skills. In S. Marshall and J. Turnbull (eds.), *Cognitive Behaviour Therapy* (pp. 121–52). London: Balliere Tindall.

Troop, N. A. and Treasure, J. L. (1997). Setting the scene for eating disorders, II: Childhood helplessness and mastery. *Psychological Medicine*, 27: 531–8.

Trower, P., Casey, A. and Dryden, W. (1988). *Cognitive Behavioural Counselling in Action*. London: Sage.

Turnbull, J. (1996). The context of therapy. In S. Marshall and J. Turnbull (eds.), *Cognitive Behaviour Therapy* (pp. 11–28). London: Balliere Tindall.

Ussher, J. (1990). Choosing psychology; or, Not throwing the baby out with the bath water. In E. Burman (ed.), *Feminists and Psychological Practice* (pp. 47–61). London: Sage.

Ward, M. (1993). Therapy as abuse. *Clinical Psychology Forum*, 54: 23–5.

Warner, R. (1994). *Recovery from Schizophrenia: Psychiatry and political economy*. London: Routledge.

Waterhouse, R. (1993). 'Wild women don't have the blues': A feminist critique of 'person-centred' counselling and therapy. *Feminism and Psychology*, 3: 55–71.

Weedon, C. (1987). *Feminist Practice and Poststructuralist Theory*. Oxford: Basil Blackwell.

Wenegrat, B. (1995). *Illness and Power: Women's mental disorders and the battle between the sexes*. London: New York University Press.

White, M. and Epston, D. (1990). *Narrative Means to Therapeutic Ends*. Adelaide: Dulwich Centre Productions.

Williams, J. and Watson, G. (1994). Mental health services that empower women: the challenge to clinical psychology. *Clinical Psychology Forum*, 64: 11–7.

Index